A TRAJECTORY OF HUMAN IMAGINATION FROM WALKING TO FLYING SAUCERS

Volume I

THINKING WHILE WALKING
Gathering Embodied Experience for Writing

A TRAJECTORY OF HUMAN IMAGINATION FROM WALKING TO FLYING SAUCERS

Volume I

THINKING WHILE WALKING
Gathering Embodied Experience for Writing

SATVIR SINGH

AUTHORSPRESS

Worldwide Circulation through Authorspress Global Network
First Published in 2023
by
Authorspress
Q-2A Hauz Khas Enclave, New Delhi-110 016 (India)
Phone: (0) 9818049852
E-mail: authorspressgroup@gmail.com
Website: www.authorspressbooks.com

A Trajectory of Human Imagination from Walking to Flying Saucers

Volume I. Thinking While Walking: Gathering Embodied Experience for Writing

ISBN 978-93-5529-953-6

Printed in India at Thomson Press (India) Limited

Acknowledgements

First and foremost, I wish to thank all-merciful God and the Holy Mother for giving me strength and inspiration to pen this work. Since the work has originally been submitted to the department of English, Punjabi University, Patiala as a Ph.D. dissertation and awarded on the 26 May 2022, the author and the publisher are grateful to Prof. Arvind, the Vice Chancellor of the Punjabi University, Patiala, for granting the permission for publication. Thanks are due to Dr. Rajesh Kumar Sharma, the supervisor, for his valuable suggestions, especially on the writing style. He has been the impetus behind successful completion of such an arduous task. I must also thank Dr. Dananjay Singh, Professor & Head of the Centre for English Studies, JNU, New Delhi, for helping me secure the visitor's card to consult Dr. B. R. Ambedkar Central Library, JNU, New Delhi. A deep sense of gratitude is due to Dr. Saroj Kumar Mahananda, Professor, Department of English, Jamia Milia Islamia, New Delhi for accepting my request to write the foreword. Last but not the least, my family, especially, my daughter, Ishpreet, deserves to be acknowledged for being a little angel of inspiration while I was typewriting the manuscript.

Satvir Singh

Foreword

With the advancement of research in the evolution of human being, one is increasingly made aware of the fact that human brain has a far closer and integral a relation with human feet than believed earlier. Now it has been established beyond doubt that bipedalism and erect posture have had revolutionary effect on the way human beings have come to use their brain and limbs. But, even before the scientific study of human anatomy proved the connection between feet and brain, celebrated philosophers and critical thinkers had realised the connection between walking and thinking. For instance, as reported in Plato's *Protagoras*, Socrates is said to have enjoyed teaching while walking and the way his disciples followed him around. Even Plato himself has been made fun of by Comedy writers for 'tiring his legs out' while making 'wise plans.' Aristotle himself was known as *peripatetic*, meaning, *someone who keeps moving from one place to another*, for his habit of strolling up and down while teaching. Pythagoras was no exception. In the more recent times Jean Jacques Rousseau, Henry David Thoreau and Charles Baudelaire have dwelt quite in detail about the significance of walking. It is in this context, the current study titled *Thinking While Walking: Gathering Embodied Experience for Writing* by Dr. Satvir Singh is a wonderful initiative to bring to the contemporary readership the rich tradition of 'the literature of walking.' Dr. Singh starts with an erudite Introduction which sets the tone of the study by outlining the theoretical ramifications of bipedalism, using the ideas of Lovejoy and Dart, tracing its impact on the evolution of the human brain and its cognitive powers. Walking, as Singh suggests, was an essential condition for and accompaniment of thinking, it is simultaneously a cultural and aesthetic act. The study establishes the links between the act of walking and the art of writing through the Romantics, the modern urban *flâneur* and the concept of Benjamin's 'ambulatory gaze.' The literature and theoretical review are rigorous and exhaustive, traversing from the ancient to the psychological and post-human. The study also locates a more postmodern response of walking as protest against the urgency of the automobile. The research problem thus branches across three levels tracing the changing nature of the relationship between the walking and the thinking subject and finally an analytical study of the literary 'walking' texts. Thereafter, the book presents an in-depth analysis of the following texts in four chapters: Jean Jacques Rousseau's *The Reverie of the Solitary Walker*, Henry David Thoreau's *Walden* and "Walking," Charles Dickens' *The Uncommercial Traveller*, Baudelaire's *The Painter of Modern Life.* Thus, we can see how Rousseau treats walking as a way to study and heal the traumatised self. And Thoreau, since he values freedom above all, practices walking in the wild which he says has the power to emancipate the walker from all bonds of ignorance. Eiseley walks to find the traces of the unknown journey of human beings down the ages as found in the fossil remains. Dicken's walking and thinking plays a vital role to situate a writer's work into the time and the place of its making. Baudelaire creates the artistic walker in the modern city whom he calls flâneur who roams and critiques the modern city. In the form of final take away, taking cue from the writers studied, the book argues that walking is not just a mundane activity but a far more holistic spiritual exercise which has the propensity to connect the present of mankind with its past and future.

This book can be a wonderful reference material for not just the researchers of 18th - 19th century literature and philosophy but also for students of cultural studies and postmodernism who face in Artificial Intelligence a far more formidable foe than ambivalence and indecisiveness and which seems to be threatening the very nature in which humankind is likely to behave in days to come.

Prof. Saroj Kumar Mahananda
Professor, Department of English
Faculty of Humanities and Languages,
Jamia Millia Islamia, New Delhi.

Contents

Introduction

> Isn't it really quite extraordinary to see that, since man took his first steps, no one has asked himself why he walks, how he walks, if he has ever walked, if he could walk better, what he achieves in walking . . . questions that are tied to all the philosophical, psychological, and political systems which preoccupy the world? (Balzac qtd. in Amato)

> Walking has been so natural and so ordinary that few thought of writing about it [...] it is only in this age, as a protest against the wheel, walking as a literary cult has come into being. (Graham qtd in Coverley 11)

> Both walking and writing are simple, common activities. You put one foot in front of the other; you put one word in front of another. What could be more basic than a single step, more basic than a single word? Yet if you connect enough of these basic building blocks, connect enough steps, enough words, you may find that you've done something quite special. The thousand-mile journey starts with the single step; the million-word manuscript starts with a single syllable. (Nicholson 256)

Walking as the Evolutionary First Step

Walking,[1] the act of putting one foot in front of another to move forward, is usually supposed to be an activity ordinary enough to be regarded unworthy of any serious thought. However, the ordinary may hide the extraordinary. The ability to walking once identified human beings amongst non-walking species. Not only has walking played a key role in the rise of hominids,[2] but it has also hidden in it the rarest secrets about the human evolutionary journey. Along with the ability to walk upright, our species are remarkable for possessing big brain relative to body size. The large brain and bipedal walking are the two strains of evolution that are so intertwined and mutually

1 Walking in this study is taken to mean not so much a locomotive activity to get from place A to place B as a cultural, aesthetic and primordial practice performed intentionally. It connects a walker with the immediate surroundings in which s/he is practising walking. In the city, he is a flâneur; in nature, he is a species amongst other species walking in the wild. Therefore, walking must be viewed in the context in which it is being practised.

2 A mammal of the family of Hominidae, which includes human beings and their fossil ancestors.

complementary that they seem to be the two sides of the same coin. However, contrary to common belief, the ability to walk and developing the big brain had been two distinct evolutionary trends in the beginning, before they collided with each other at the point of the female pelvis (Zollikofer qtd. in Costandi). In fact, the pelvis is the point of conflict of three fundamental streaks of evolution: bipedal walking, parturition and thermoregulation. The early human ancestors had a brain of the size of an ape, yet their fossil remains show signs of bipedality. Their adoption of this difficult act of standing upright on two legs has something to do with the conclusions of the savanna theory[3] that bipedality facilitated a higher vantage point to cast a wider glance at the surroundings, less exposure to the heat of the sun and freed hands for carrying food and young ones over long distances (Kaas).

Human ancestors had been bipedal walkers before the brain started expanding rapidly (Fischer and Mitteroeckerb). Upright walking on the two feet – which might have been necessitated by a different set of survival pressures – instead of augmenting the brain expansion presented a challenge. The dynamics of walking as well as imperatives of thermoregulation demanded a total reconfiguration of the pelvic anatomy to make it bipedally efficient, and of suitable dimensions to be able to regulate temperature (Gruss and Schmitt). In addition, the female pelvis, at the same time, had to be broad enough to be able to deliver big-brained broad-shouldered babies. This is known as the obstetric dilemma (Washburn qtd. in "Childbirth," *Wittyfeed*), which is the result of the collision of expanding brain and narrowing birth canals due to the imperatives set by bipedal walking and thermoregulation. To meet the demands of upright walking, the pelvis underwent some significant modifications: first, it became narrow – it has to dilate three times its normal size to

---

3 The savanna theory is one of the oldest hypotheses to explain the birth of bipedalism. The savanna theory postulates that the early hominids, under various evolutionary pressures, left the trees for the open savanna where they had to walk erect for the advantages it offered over walking on all fours: the erect posture enabled bipeds to watch for prey as well as for predators over the tall shrubs. Moreover, it requires comparatively less energy to walk bipedally.

See. Ko, Kwang Hyun. "Origins of Bipedalism." *Brazilian Archives of Biology and Technology*, Vol. *58*, No.6, pp.929-934, 2015, https://doi.org/10.1590/S1516-89132015060399

give birth; second, it got twisted by ninety degrees in the middle so that a foetus has to rotate through the varying dimensions of the female cervical canal to exit. This is known as "rotational birth" (Gruss and Schmitt), unique in human beings.

In contrast, the birth canal of the quadruped primates is described as being straight and of consistent width. To resolve the obstetric dilemma, the evolutionary forces came up with the solution of open fontanel bones that overlap to facilitate the passage of the head through the relatively tighter and twisted birth canal. After birth, the bones remain open for an initial couple of years when the brain sees rapid expansion, and, then, they close up and fuse together to seal the head. The closure is known as the metopic suture. It was the evolution of metopic suture that corrected the collision course of walking and large brain, and set them parallel to each other as mutually complementary processes.

This event of bipedal walking and expanding brain was no less a revolution in evolution that set the tone for the ever-faster growth of the human brain. Thus, the development and organisation of the human brain have been dictated by a narrowing pelvis, which, in turn, was being modified to facilitate bipedal walking. Therefore, the two evolutionary strains of bipedal walking and expanding brain merged with one another, and, then, they were resurrected in an altogether new shape and structure, which were favourable to both the strains. To quote Mo Costandi, "A new analysis of the skull suggests that human brain evolution may have been shaped by changes in the female reproductive system that occurred when our ancestors stood upright."

There has been a long-drawn controversy between the scholars about whether big brain or bipedal walking evolved first. It is, therefore, imperative to cast a cursory glance over the chronology and significance of the available fossil evidence, which led to the resolution of the disagreement in favour of bipedal walking. Today, we have clinching evidence to conclude that bipedal walking came earlier than the development of big brain. Thus, Lovejoy observes, "bipedalism was one of the first hallmarks of the hominin lineage" (118). However, for a long time, scholars studying human evolution had presumed that big brain came first, then the ability to make tools, and the bipedal mode of walking was the overall result of these changes. However, the fossil records discovered over the last twenty years tell a different story. As per archaeological evidence, australopithecines,[4] our earliest known ancestors who lived three million years ago, had neither big brain nor the capacity to make tools. However, their fossil remains clearly manifest many peculiarities of bipedal walking. "Bipedality," he argues further," accompanied a set of behavioural adaptations that became the key evolutionary innovation of humanity's earliest ancestors" (Lovejoy 118). Moreover, it was bipedalism related "behavioural adaptations" (118) that set the stage for the fast-track evolution of hominids.

Lovejoy is not the only one to make the above observation. Raymond Dart agrees with Lovejoy in saying that bipedalism evolved first, the bigger brain followed. After examining the fossil skull called *Taung Child*, he proposed that bipedalism evolved before relatively larger brain. In 1924, the first Australopithecine fossil skull, known as the *Taung Child*, was found in a limestone quarry near Taung in South Africa. The skull was of an infant of about three or four years who lived on this earth 2.5 million years ago. Taxonomically, it is related to the species named *Au. africanus* and had a brain size similar to that of a modern chimpanzee. The positioning of the foramen magnum, Dart argued, suggested that the Taung Child was bipedal. The hypothesis proposed by Dart that "bipedalism evolved before larger brain" (qtd. in "Bipedalism") posed a fundamental challenge to the views held by the majority of scholars at his time. It was widely contradicted partly because of its limited sample size and the fragmentary condition of fossil evidence.

The debate and research about the exact timeline of bipedalism and brain size took another fifty years to settle down. The discovery of the fossilised skeleton of a female dating 3.2 million years in 1974 proved beyond doubt that bipedalism came earlier than the big brain. The skeleton was named Lucy, was remarkable in terms of having a relatively smaller brain and clearly noticeable features of bipedalism. It was discovered by Donald Johanson in 1974. Though the timeline of bipedalism is still under revision as more fossils are discovered,

---

4. Any of various extinct hominids (genera Australopithecus and Paranthropus) that existed two to four million years ago in southern and eastern Africa and included gracile and robust forms exhibiting bipedal locomotion, near-human dentition, and relatively small brain.

   See, Merriam-Webster Dictionary. https://www.merriam-webster.com/dictionary/australopithecine

there is no doubt that it was bipedalism that set the stage for the faster evolution of human ancestors. ("Bipedalism")

One game-changing edge that bipedalism offered was the freeing of forelimbs, which paved the way for the invention of stone tools – the birth of technology. There seems to be a consensus amongst the anthropologist on 'the notion that "freeing the hands" for tool-using, weapon-handling, food-gathering, and self-defense (sic) was the main cause of hominid bipedalism' (Hewes 693). This, in turn, led to the development and use of more and more complex tools for hunting wild animals and gathering food. The year-round availability of a high protein diet by cooking and preserving it helped provide for the nutrition demands of the expanding brain (Kaas). The lifting of telescopic head to survey the landscape around from a vantage point put evolutionary pressure on the corresponding areas in the cerebral cortex of the brain; hence, these areas saw maximum expansion (Falk). By taking to bipedal walking, the nose was lifted to a height where it was no longer required to be as sensitive as it used to be in a quadruped: the function of the nose diminished (Freud 19n14). Alternatively, the brain areas catering to the other sensory and motor functions such as vision, hearing etc., and analytical centres processing sensory stimuli saw explosive development.

Thus, it can be argued that during the entire trajectory of human evolution, it was the human brain that not only tripled in size but also significantly reconfigured itself in terms of evolution of the cerebral cortex. The intricate surface of the cerebral cortex, which contains more than eighty-five per cent of total brain mass, has been positioned over the core of the brain. Cerebral cortex, the most recently developed uppermost layer of the brain, not only performs complex cognitive functions such as thinking, reasoning, language etc., but it is also responsible for carrying out voluntary tasks such as processing sensory information controlling motor functions etc.

Though the question of exactly what had happened before human ancestors had to scramble to two feet is yet to be fully answered, what happened after they learned to walk upright as a way of life stands satisfactorily explained. Walking upright on two legs by human beings is not simply a means of locomotion; it is a complex gravity-defying posture achieved with "unending skeletomuscular adjustment[s]" (Skoyles 1061). By learning to walk like this under whatever selection pressures, human beings seem to have re-directed the pace of evolution beyond any of their fellow non-walking primates. Lovejoy observes, "The development of erect walking may have been a crucial initiating event in human evolution" (Lovejoy).

Thus, not only the positioning of the cerebral cortex but the very origin of it was dictated by bipedal walking. To quote Leisman et al., "Bipedalism served as a significant basis for the evolution of the human neocortex." If it has so directly originated out of bipedal walking, then it must be intimately connected with the pair of legs. Cortical areas, argues John R.Skoyles, processing the spatial and other cognitions needed to enable vertical balance [while walking bipedally] was an essential reason for brain size expansion of *Homo erectus*" (Summary, 1060). Human beings are the only upright-walking species on the planet with a special skill to harness gravitational forces in their favour, making walking the most efficient mode of locomotion (Wayman). This was the outcome of "genetic mutation" (Leisman et al.) spread over a long span of time. This evolutionary process – resulting in larger neural networks – helped us to develop synchronicity between the motor system and rhythmic foot movement in walking. The same neural networks finally resulted in "cognitive binding and consciousness" (Leisman et al.). Leisman and others finally argue that thinking function evolved because of and parallel to the evolution of human upright walking. To quote, "complex motoricity and cognition are functionally connected, and both evolved in parallel, interdependently" (Leisman et al.). It can thus be argued that walking and thinking are so organically connected with each other that one cannot happen without the other. Having said that, it ought to be stated that I do not argue that one cannot think at all while being in any other posture such as sitting or lying down than upright walking; one can surely think while being in numerous other postures and positions – astronauts can think even while floating in a spacecraft in the space. How their thinking is conditioned by the peculiarity of the place in which they are can be the subject of a separate research work. But what is being argued here is that walking enables experiential thinking, which is remarkable in terms of engaging the body and mind of the walker not only with each other in perfect harmony but also helps him establish a connection with the place through which the walker is walking in a way that no other means of travelling can do. Therefore, the present project is confined to studying the relation between walking and thinking with reference to certain prominent authors, thinkers, philosophers and their works. Walking has been so myriad in its manifestation in each generation that there have appeared as many varieties of walking as there are situations in which walking is being performed. To quote Wylie on the varieties of walking,

> ...there is no such thing as 'walking-in-itself,' no certain physical motion which is, as it were, elementary, universal and pure. There are only varieties of walking, whether these be discursive registers (pilgrimage, courtship, therapy, exercise, protest) or particular modes of engagement (strolling, hiking, promenading, pacing, herding, guiding, marching). (235)

Walking as an Essential Accompaniment to Thinking

The peculiarity of walking consists in the uniquely embodied experience it offers to the walker. Such experience is unique to the person and yet embedded in the place. It has received varied representation in the works of the writers since the eighteenth century. At first glance, it can be regarded from two perspectives: historical and philosophical. Though the tradition of walking and thinking goes back to Greek philosophers, the modern practice of walking and *thinking about walking* (italics mine) begins with J. J. Rousseau in France. Greek philosophers walked and philosophised, but they did not philosophise on the act of walking. However, in ancient Greece, the practice of walking was all-pervasive. Walking was not only recognised as a background to the philosophical conversation, but it was also incorporated in Greek architecture as an essential part of daily life (Kissin). Because of their walking culture, almost every school of Greek philosophers – the Peripatetics, the Stoics, the Sophists to mention a few – regarded walking as the necessary background for thinking. Later, in France, Rousseau's *Reveries of the Solitary Walker* (1782) emerges as one of the treatises on the dynamics of thinking and walking. The experience of walking seems to have provided him with access to hitherto inaccessible recesses of his "self." It seems to have given him the position of a walker, having the two feet firmly placed on the ground, from which he could write (Solnit 21). Rousseau might have said, "I walk; therefore, I am."

The act of walking has been a natural companion of thinking on profound issues by thinkers such as Plato, Nietzsche, Thoreau, Emerson and others. For Thoreau, walking is no less than an act of spiritual meditation that lets one attain a heightened state of awareness of oneself and the surroundings. Quite radically, he urges humankind to cast aside the modern life of drudgery for a life of purity, freedom and awakening (Thoreau 168). Dickens enjoins walking for its promise of a pure, unadulterated experience of people and places, and, for revisiting memories with the profound awareness that the memories one is leaving behind would someday be retraced by another walker. Related to this is Baudelaire's concept of *flâneur*, who walks in the city to capture the fleeting beauty of the present with a keen, observant and philosophical eye. He shuns the "artificial busyness" (Stephen, "Flâneur") of modern city life to enjoy a leisurely amble in the very midst of the urban hustle and bustle. Walking, for Loren Eiseley, takes the form of hikes to reach far-flung places to study the pre-historic sites and fossilised objects that offer him an insight into the long and layered mystery of evolution.

The history of the literature of walking is the root, while the philosophy is the fruit. There are writers that deal with the historical and evolutionary aspects of walking, and there are writers who have written on the cultural and philosophical aspects of walking. Such writing is growing into a genre in its own right that has also been termed "pedestrian canon" (Coverley 14). The works of these writers offer us a range of instances amounting to a tentative framework to study different shades of the literature of walking – how to practise walking and the various ways to creatively express the experience of walking into literature. Their writings show many nuances of walking, such as the historically changing human engagement with the world, a rediscovery of walking as a medium not only to connect with the social and natural environment but also a way of going inward to the deepest recesses of the self; walking as a tool to gather first hand creative raw material from around the world, and walking as a way into an epiphanic awareness of the inner and outer reality and so on. So, with the insights offered by these writers, it is proposed to study the above-mentioned texts to examine the modern subjects' origins as a walking thinker and writer. Following is a brief overview of what such prominent writers offer to a serious reader that also provides the tentative framework for our interpretive approach.

The Emergence of Walking as a Cultural and Aesthetic Act

While most of the walking happens in the realm of the mundane and quotidian, to invest it with aesthetic and philosophical overtones is arguably a relatively recent phenomenon. Walking is the natural way the body moves about, and its rhythm makes it one with the involuntary rhythms of the human body, such as breathing and the beating of the heart. It is the threshold between doing something and doing nothing. It works the body, awakens the senses to register the environmental stimuli and frees the mind to connect and think. Walking is the natural pace at which the human body and mind are biologically attuned. Rebecca Solnit notes, "walking allows us to be in our bodies and in the world without being made busy by them" (11). Indeed, no other means of locomotion except walking lets one have a sense of place[5] (Solnit). Merlin Coverley makes a similar observation that walking always had in it the potential to harmonise mind and body so that diverse thoughts begin to form themselves into a kind of cohesiveness that can be tapped by a creative writer to enrich his/her work. To quote, "[f]or millennia the act of walking and the bodily rhythms it incorporates have been felt to somehow reflect or engender the mental processes of abstract thought, as if the metronomic beat of the walker's step could mark time, shaping the thoughts it provokes into a coherent narrative" (12). But Merlin Coverley misses the power of walking to root the thought in the place which then leads to experiential thought instead of "abstract thought" as opined by Coverley. It can, thus, be argued that walking not only enables a wholesomeness between the mind and the body but also lets the mind-body collective register the place and thus form a triangular ensemble of the mind, the body and the place. Moreover, the thoughts thus produced are felt thoughts by the mind-body collective, and, at the same time, they are rooted in the place in profound ways.

How a walk can shape thinking and writing and how it can be written into a literary work was demonstrated by Rousseau. Walking can provide a shape and structure to a work of literature; walking has inspired works that are interdisciplinary and digressive, with the narrative put together associatively rather than chronologically. After Rousseau, Wordsworth let his walks be his poems. For him walking was an aesthetic pilgrimage from which he gathered themes and characters for his poetry. The language and versification of his compositions owe their rhythm and cadences to the rhythm of his walks in the Lake District.

---

5 The sense of place is the ability to experience a place with one's senses, which can only be done through walking on two feet because walking provides the right pace at which human senses are designed to work. Also, the sense of place includes the local oral stories/myths associated with that particular place over a period of time. Only walking could enable one to interact with the local people who narrate the stories.

In the nineteenth century, the Romantics were not the only ones who walked; there was another kind of walker in the city. The industrial society, much criticised by the Romantics like Wordsworth, created a new form of walking, urban walking. The urban pedestrians, unlike Wordsworth, have to walk out of sheer necessity, under the surveillance of various kinds, through the congested city lanes, on the sidewalks, avoiding whizzing traffic, to commute to and from the workplace. Their concerns, far from being literary and aesthetic, were practical and utilitarian. They had no time to absorb the sense of place by hanging around, zooming in on sights and scenes around himself, running into oddly interesting walkers and conversing with them, visiting the ruins of history which had been mapped out of the "conscious of the city."[6] This lack was supplied by the Paris born, intellectual-looking, bohemian stroller – the *flâneur*. The marathon walker, frequenter of fashionable places, keen-eyed observer and having some degree of literary pretensions, the *flâneur* became the interpreter of modern city life (Benjamin 806).

The notion of *flâneur* finds its first mention in Baudelaire's *Painter of Modern Life* (1863). Baudelaire considered him (as *flâneur* is a masculine noun in French) as an "observer, philosopher…the painter of the passing moment and of all the suggestions of eternity" in it (5). Monsieur G., on whom the notion of *flâneur* has been modelled, says Baudelaire, is a "pure poetic hypothesis, conjecture, a labour of the imagination" (6). He is an avid traveller/walker and a "cosmopolitan" (6) who has left his home to make everywhere his home. Since he is a "man of the world" (7) and a spiritual citizen of the universe, he wants to know and understand everything that happens not only in the world but also in the universe. Whereas an artist lives a very limited life, the *flâneur* being a man of the world feels at home everywhere, yet belongs nowhere. Among other things, the genius of *flâneur* consists of an uncanny ability to recover childhood at will while being an adult for all other intents and purposes – he is a "man-child" (8). This means he has the ability to erase at will the cognitive conditioning that he has undergone since childhood and to look at everything with childlike wonder. Hence, he

---

6 The "conscious of the city" here refers to the Freudian view of the human mind as the conscious and the unconscious. Here it refers to those areas of the city that are not ordinarily noticed as they are hidden from the eye of those people, especially tourists, who travel through the usual city road network.

can observe everything in a "state of newness" and is "always drunk" (8). Besides being a grown-up child, he has an acute sensitivity to things sublime. In him, this hypersensitivity manifests itself as a kind of "nervous shock" at the sight of something sublime; the shock gets conveyed to the "core of the brain" (8) where, by degrees, it gets illumined into a "diadem of dazzling clarity" (Baudelaire, "Benediction" 15) which finally leads to a creative outlet. Baudelaire further says any aesthetic phenomenon is made up of two components: the transient, manifest present, and, the immutable, latent eternal (13). It is precisely this transient, fleeting element of the present that Baudelaire calls "modernity." Thus, the *flâneur* has the task cut out for him: to extract "poetry from history" and to sift "the eternal from the transitory" (12). Without the artistic ability to distil and express this "transitory, fugitive element" in the "present," the beauty of the eternal is indeterminable (13). In short, the job of the *flâneur* is to sift the eternal from the phantasmagoria of the present flux. Moreover, when Baudelaire was pondering over the notion of *flâneur*, someone else was already practising it as an artistic tool. As mentioned already, Victor Fournel, writing with reference to Dickens's narrator in *The Uncommercial Traveller* (qtd. in Tyler 14), maintains that "*badaud*" (who is also a walker/traveller much like *flâneur*) sheds his identity to mix up with the crowd; but on the contrary, *flâneur*, says Fournel, does keep his identity in firm possession. However, it is easy to infer that although Baudelaire's *flâneur* loves to be amidst the masses incognito, it does not mean he sheds his identity altogether. It is not his external identity that undergoes a change: rather, he spiritually orientates himself to become a "child" who experiences everything as if he is experiencing it for the first time. He does not slough off his identity altogether as *Badaud* does, but he definitely does assume a collective narratorial perspective (sheds "I" to embrace "we") to suit his needs for mixing up in the crowd. This is exactly what the *badaud* does. Tyler further writes that Dickens's narrative persona in *The Uncommercial Traveller* is a descendant of the semi-autobiographical narrator of periodicals such as *The Spectator*, *The Idler*, *The Rambler* and others (13). Therefore, it is more versatile than *flâneur*. At times, the narrator becomes critical and censoring like a sanitation inspector, for instance, when he happens to visit an eatery for the working classes in the essay ("The Boiled Beef of New England"); sometimes, he holds back his personality altogether and focuses on journalistic reporting as in

"The Shipwreck;" at times, he chooses to mingle so completely with the crowd that he becomes indistinguishable from it, as in "Two Views of a Cheap Theatre" when Dickens assumes the point of view of the audience: "[w]e were a motley assemblage of people, and we had a good many boys and young men among us; we also had many girls and young women (Dickens 88).

The essay entitled "Poor Mercantile Jack" records his night wanderings as a police squad member hunting for the swindlers who have laid traps for "poor Jack."[7] There is a play of the point of view between the general and the particular as sometimes Jack seems to be a particular person and sometimes a faceless sailor. As in his seemingly aimless rambles, especially the present one during the night, Dickens is in the process of searching for the person as well as the point of view from which to narrate his story. In the essay "Wapping Workhouse," Dickens states his peculiar style of wandering: "… having lost my way, and, abandoning myself to the narrow streets in a Turkish frame of mind, [I] relied on predestination to bring me somehow or other to the place I wanted, if I were ever to get there (25)? Dickens's words are echoed by W.G. Sebald when he states his manner of reaching the desired place by walking in an unplanned way. Sebald writes a century and a half later, "If you look at a dog following the advice of his nose, he traverses a patch of land in a completely unplottable manner. And he invariably finds what he's looking for. I think that, as I've always had dogs, I've learned from them how to do this" ("Conversations," Sebald 94).

Walter Benjamin took the idea of *flâneur* from Baudelaire's collection of poems *The Flowers of Evil.* According to Benjamin, Baudelaire's poems are a creative record of what strikes "the ambulatory gaze" (qtd. in Friedberg 5) that the *flâneur* casts on contemporary Parisian cityscape. Benjamin does not only write about *flâneur* in his magnum opus *The Arcades Project* (1982) but also writes it as a *flâneur* (Seal); furthermore, his way of researching and collecting his material (observing the contemporary scene, taking down

---

7 Poor Mercantile Jack is a character in the essay of the same title in the anthology of essays. *The Uncommercial Traveller* (1860) by Charles Dickens. While distinguishing between *flâneur* and Baudelaire Victor Fournel explains that *flâneur* is a critical observer while *badaud* is a curious gaper, a rubberneck bystander (Shaya 46) and a part of the crowd. Whereas *flâneur* always keeps his individuality, the individuality of a *badaud* disappears.

fragmentary notes) has come from a walker's glance on the world around him. So in *The Arcades Project*, a practising *flâneur* writes about a theoretical *flâneur.* While dwelling on the psychological effect that the overwhelming sensory stimuli offered by a city have on its citizens, Benjamin brings up two concepts, *Erlebnis* and *Erfahrung*; the former refers to sensory numbness produced by a baffling mélange of sights, sounds and smells, the latter to the pace of cruising movement through the cityscape, and having to experience the city only at that pace. For Benjamin, the combined effect of these two was confusion and alienation in the mind of the city dweller. The faster the kaleidoscope of images, sounds, and smells flows into the consciousness, and the more alert the consciousness is to register it, the lesser do they penetrate experience and memory (Benjamin, "Illuminations"). It is at this point that walking, the slowing down of movement, the leisurely lingering over the scenes and places that catch the eye, stands out in all its importance. The *flâneur* sauntering at a relaxed pace is able to spend as much time over the sight or scene of interest as he wishes to. The slowing down is a challenge to the imperative of life at a fast pace. At the walking pace, the eye can linger on an object, figure out the coherence and contradictions, and, so work out the buried connections/fissures between the apparent diversity/unity of a city. A *Flâneur* imagines the modern scene in a subversive way because he has time for a free run of imagination. Therefore, in a way, his subversive walking aided by imagination deconstructs modernity and creates new wholes from fragments. To the *flâneur,* the dreamlike atmosphere offered by a city is a site of excitement, and a meeting point of many realms of human experience. It is the kaleidoscopic cultural reality of the city, rather than the human psyche, that provides "false consciousness" in the "collective *un*conscious" where memories: conscious, unconscious, past and present meet to form a dreamlike "reality" (Buck-Morss 109).

Flânerie in the feminine engages Lauren Elkin in her book *Flâneuse: Women Walk the City in Paris, New York, Tokyo, Venice, and London.* In her book, Elkin questions the masculine representation of *flâneur* in the arcades of the literary and social history of France, England and America. She asks whether a woman could be a street stroller. Her answer is not only an emphatic "yes" but also that such a woman city walker really has a historical presence. She coins the title *flâneuse*, which is a feminine term for *flâneur*. She argues, "To suggest that there couldn't be a female version of the flâneur is to limit the ways women have interacted with the city to the ways men have interacted with the city." (Elkin)

Elkin builds up her argument with reference to two iconic female literary figures – Jean Rhys in Paris, Virginia Woolf in London – who also practised *flânerie*[8] in their own ways. Her book is path-breaking in terms of offering a feminine perspective on walking. Elkin puts up a solid case against the masculine monopoly of the cultural practice of *flânerie*. Its critique of *flâneur* is subversive as well as informative about the representation of women on the city roads in the same historical period as that of *flâneur*. It is like a walking tour through literary and cultural history, biography, literary criticism and so on, challenging male dominance on the lanes of history.

Since very ancient times, walking has played the role of a catalyst to let the internal and the external landscapes interact, shaping not only human imagination but also the physical landscapes. It has made its way through wild growth, discovered walkaways, led to the construction of roads and trade routes, connected the local with the global, created a sense of place from a landscape; it has shaped and has got shaped by the architecture of the cities and parks; it has spawned a vast corpus of walking stories and poems, narratives, of pilgrimages, mountaineering expeditions and travelogues (Solnit 68-69). Though the literature of walking seems to be older than history, it is yet to be recognised as a distinct genre. Often categorised under titles such as "descriptive poetry," "nature poetry" or at best "travel literature," the literature of walking cannot be adequately described by these labels. To give the literature of walking its due place in literature, there is a need to study such writing on its own terms. We may call such literature significant insofar as it can offer unprecedented encounters with an important part of the experience. Further, stressing the subversive potential of walking, Merlin Coverley in *The Art of Wandering: The Writer as Walker* says that walking seems to be antithetical to the very spirit of the modern city as the city is synonymous with faster transportation. Coverley's work is the latest of all previous accounts of walking. Coverley corrals writers not as per the genre or historical period but according to their walking preferences. He says that the literature of walking is

8 *Flânerie* is a gender-neutral noun, which designates the practice of city wandering by both the sexes.

assuming the form of a "pedestrian canon" (14). His way of organising walkers in subsets, such as walker as a writer, walker as a philosopher, walker as a pilgrim, walker as a vagrant, walker vis-à-vis natural world, walker as visionary, the *flâneur* and so on is indeed innovative. In fact, walking provides lived, a human perspective that allows one to go beyond the official representation of the city by discovering new paths to explore and experience hidden and obscure places on the map, not only on the margins but sometimes in the heart of the city also.

The relationship between walking and writing is the central concern of Rebecca Solnit's *Wanderlust: A History of Walking*. Though Solnit refers to the Greek culture of walking and philosophising, her book does not so much deal with the history of walking as with walking as a cultural act. The emergent practice of walking, she says, is a response to the sense of disembodiment in contemporary life due to automation and urbanisation. She rightly observes that the subject as conceptualised by contemporary theory is an abstract and passive human body. It has been allowed only the erotic and bodily functions to pretend a semblance of life. Though Solnit includes the poems of Wordsworth and memoirs of Rousseau and others as examples of literature featuring the walking body in its natural pre-industrial form as an answer to the problem of disembodiment, her book is a partially finished project.

Joseph Amato's *On Foot: A History of Walking* traces the trajectory of walking from originally being a compulsory activity to now being merely a choice and pastime in developed countries. He charts a history of walkers and their practice of walking down the ages, including such figures as Rousseau, Thoreau and Wordsworth. He also deals with the changing cultural signification of the act of walking at different ages. Deploring the commodification of walking in the age of capitalism, Amato aptly says that walking is still the "heart of human life and movement." Finally, Amato states that walking and humanity are synonymous; if there is no walking, there can be no humanity at all.

Frederic Gros's *A Philosophy of Walking* is different from the above two in terms of its dealing not with the history, nor culture, but the idea of walking. For Gros, walking is more of a spiritual quest than a practical activity undertaken to cover a distance between two points; it is a way to commune with the sublime in nature. Gros's walker leaves civilisation far behind. The putting of one step ahead of another, says Gros, has transformative powers. The act of coming down on earth, in fact, raises one above the mundane reality so that one comes to shed one's societal identity to experience oneness with the universe. Harking back to the Hindu and the Buddhist philosophies, Gros remarks that walking is a way to spiritual enlightenment as well. A galaxy of thinkers and philosophers such as Nietzsche, Rousseau, Rimbaud, Thoreau and Wordsworth owed their creative ideas to extensive walking in the wild. Despite his personal distaste for walking in the city, Gros admits that *flâneur* – who is a sophisticated city walker and a product of the culture of walking in the city of Paris – is an emergent form of walking in the contemporary age.

Geoff Nicholson, in *The Lost Art of Walking: The History, Science, Philosophy, and Literature of Pedestrianism*, touches upon some significant aspects of walking, such as walking and human evolution and, the Greek tradition of walking and philosophising. Citing clinical evidence on foetuses that start making walking motions even when their cortex is not fully formed, Nicholson argues that walking is a brainless activity. Further, he shows that the English language can describe the numerous shades of walking with high precision. He quotes tens of descriptive words and phrases. Nicholson introduces Psychogeography as an emerging area of study; it combines the act of walking with the insights of psychology and geography to study the effects of geographic environment on the human mind.

Nicholson views Romantic walking as a unique act in a number of ways. The Romantics, he says, by foregrounding the simplest act of putting one foot in front of another, registered their deviance and difference from the contemporary state of affairs; Wordsworth, Blake, Dickens stand out prominently among them.

Pico Iyer in "Dead Man Walking" regards Sebald as a travel writer. He says that Sebald inverts the very foundation of the genre of travel writing, i.e. travelling for delight and adventure as a kind of escape from the immediate. Iyer remarks that the classic travel writer goes on a quest, but Sebald runs away from something, yet he repetitively and compulsively returns to the "something" he is running away from. He is so overpowered by the return of the uncanny that on his distant travels, whomsoever he meets with, he projects his inner states of mind onto him and virtually recreates the very world he is travelling to avoid, and the re-creation is profounder and deeper. Iyer's ideas coincide with those of Summers-Bremner in

"Reading Walking, Mourning: Sebald's Peripatetic Fictions." To quote Bremner: "Sebald's fictions [contain] a circular structure of mourning an object that is never named, because that object is the subject itself once its affections fail to save it: a lost cause" (304). Only death releases the subject from such a deep trauma. Iyer notices that despite all the conscientious efforts by the writer to fix his experience to reality with the help of such anchors as travel tickets, photographs, restaurant receipts, paradoxically, "the scraps serve only to intensify the sense of placelessness and silence" (59).

Rosanne Kennedy proposes to read *The Rings of Saturn* by W. G. Sebald as a posthuman work. Critical of anthropocentric roots of the humanistic tradition, posthumanism invites humanities scholars to rethink the place of human beings in relation to non-human others vis-à-vis the planet. Kennedy proposes that the literature of memoir and walking as practice contains the seeds of an alternative recognition of human beings as not autonomous but embedded in the natural and physical world. The field of life-writing studies (autobiography being the most prominent), ever since its emergence during the Enlightenment has concerned itself with narrating the development of a unique self. Now it is increasingly felt that the presumed human autonomy having its roots in the Enlightenment has resulted from privileging one term of the binary. Instead of focussing exclusively on the human subject as in autobiography/biography, Sebald's walking memoirs portray human beings as dependent on other species and the natural world around them.

Eluned Summers-Bremner reads Sebald's works in the light of Freud's and Lacan's theories of Psychoanalysis. The fact that the walking narrators of Sebald, instead of seeing the world, are themselves seen by the landscape, fits well with Lacan's idea that by becoming the object of the gaze of the rest of the world, the subject seals the possibility of completing the mourning. She says that both Lacan and Sebald are concerned with the same subject matter: human suffering in the form of trauma, which is inexpressible in language. Sebald's literary works mourn a past traumatic event by creating an atmosphere that is neither past nor present. She refers to the Freudian-Lacanian premise that failure to mourn the loss of the love object leads to melancholia that might last until death. She also refers to Linda Belau's reframing of Lacan's premise that trauma, being unrepresentable in the symbolic, returns to write itself on the body of the subject in the form of physical symptoms. Trauma in Sebald, she observes, is "elaborated through the alterations and dislocations of readerly perspective performed by memory, visual and architectural technologies old and new, and walking."

With scrutiny of several works by writers from diverse ages, lands, and cultures, one finds a surprisingly high degree of significant coincidence of walking and thinking as complementary acts. Based on the above framework, a study of the aforementioned texts can prove pioneering with respect to the changing dialectics of the human experience of walking, thinking and writing since Rousseau's experiment in form of *Reveries of the Solitary Walker.*

Literary and Creative Potential of Walking: Studying the Writing Walkers

The unique ability to walk upright has accompanied humankind in their journey down the millennia to the present. It was but obvious for such a universal human act to have played some kind of role in one of the greatest human aesthetic achievements – literature. As readers, what we receive is the finished product of literature, be that a novel, a short story, a drama, a poem or an epic. The common reader hardly ever inquiries into the conditions of its making. However, it is here that walking often plays an anonymous but vital role; walking has usually been an activity behind the scenes, with barely any presence visible clearly in the text. Of course, certain works of literature have also represented walking in so prominent a way that walking not only appears in the text as such but also becomes a structure, a motif and a conduit, so much so that there emerges a pattern that deserves in-depth study. Representations of the experience of walking in the world, as well as the way the world is experienced while walking, have undergone dramatic transformations down the ages. It should, therefore, be interesting and significant to study the historical trajectory of the practice of walking as it appears in the works of certain important writers from around the world in the last two centuries.

The word "walking," with roots in Anglo-Saxon English, means "to roll about and toss"[9] as if floating on water, hinting that organic life's may have emerged from the sea. Loren Eiseley expresses the same opinion with the authority of a practising palaeontologist:

---

9 See Oxford English Dictionary.

> …it is calcium, carbonate of lime. Why? Only because of its history. Elements more numerous than calcium in the earth's crust could have been used to build the skeleton. Our history is the reason – we came from the water. It was there the cells took the lime habit, and they kept it after we came ashore. (*Journey* Eiseley)

Over the ages, walking has been undertaken as a means of locomotion from one place to another. Bipedalism conditioned the lives of hominids and their relationship to the environment. They abandoned arboreal existence for a walking life on earth. On foot, they could tap the natural resources for their survival in a far better way. Moreover, freed hands enabled hominids to carry food, their young ones and tools during long journeys, which enabled them to migrate over long distances.

Placing one foot ahead of another to move forward is the simplest, commonest and oldest of all human activities. Yet this ordinary and neglected act of walking marked a watershed in the history of human evolution when our ancestors walked their way from their fellow species to become the masters of the planet. Unwritten anywhere in history books, the hi(story) of walking writes itself on human anatomy (Amato 21). Walking on two feet might have necessitated an erect posture that reshaped the human pelvis and limbs. The freed hands and the raised head led to the exploration of surroundings and holding, examining and using objects as tools. The anatomy shaped by bipedalism not only set hominids apart from other species in terms of posture but also allowed them "to make a fuller use of their breath and vocal chords, (sic) enabling them to issue more complex and diverse sounds than their sniffing and panting cousins…" (Amato 21).

The ability to walk seems to have acted as a precondition for developing the competence for speech. The rhythms of walking might have led to the making of accompanying sounds that eventually assumed the form of language and song. Amato quotes Robert Provine, who speculates, "hominids had to walk before they could talk" (Amato 21). He further observes, significantly, that perhaps this song and rhyme evolved not only to sustain them on their long walks across landscapes but allowed them to weave narratives about the places they visited. Bipedal locomotion seems to have produced the conditions for human beings to develop the capacity to walk and talk at the same time and, also, for the creation of song and story (Amato 22). Tim Ingold talks about "the intimate relationship between becoming knowledgeable, walking along, and the experience of weather" (121). By the "experience of weather," Ingold obviously means the mood of nature at the time of walking. Following are some of the writers whose works have been studied and reviewed as under.

Rebecca Solnit's *Wanderlust: A History of Walking* deals with the history of walking as a cultural act. She looks at walking in the contemporary age as a response to the disembodied experience brought about by automation and urbanisation. She very rightly observes that this disembodied/abstract experience forms the basis of contemporary theory.

Joseph Amato's *On Foot: A History of Walking* follows the course of walking from a compulsory activity in the past to a choice and pastime now in some countries. He looks at walking as practised by certain famous writers and thinkers such as Rousseau, Thoreau and Wordsworth. He also dwells on the cultural representation and meaning of the practice of walking at different ages.

Frederic Gros's *A Philosophy of Walking* is different from the above two in terms of its dealing not with the history, nor culture, but the philosophy of walking. For Gros, walking is more of a spiritual quest than a practical activity undertaken to cover a distance between two points; it is a way to commune with the sublime in nature. Gros's walker leaves civilisation far behind.

Geoff Nicholson, in *The Lost Art of Walking: The History, Science, Philosophy, and Literature of Pedestrianism*, touches upon some significant aspects of walking, such as walking and human evolution and the Greek tradition of walking and philosophising. Citing clinical evidence on foetuses that start making walking motions even when their cortex is not fully formed, Nicholson argues that walking is a brainless activity. Further, Psychogeography, notes Nicholson, is an emerging area of study; it combines the act of walking with the insights of psychology and geography to study the effects of geographic environment on the human mind.

Merlin Coverley's *The Art of Wandering: The Writer as Walker* is the latest of all previous accounts of walking. Coverley corrals writers not as per the genre or historical period but according to their walking preferences. He says that the literature of walking is assuming the form of a "pedestrian canon" (14). His way of organising walkers in subsets, such as walker as a writer, walker as a philosopher, walker as a pilgrim, walker as a vagrant, walker vis-à-vis natural world, walker as a visionary, a *flâneur* and so on is indeed innovative. Coverley, in this book, discusses the entire gamut of cultural representations of walking in literature down the ages.

Pico Iyer in "Dead Man Walking" regards Sebald as a travel writer. He says that Sebald inverts the very foundation of the genre of travel writing, i.e. travelling for delight and adventure as a kind of escape from the immediate. Iyer remarks that the classic travel writer goes on a quest, but Sebald runs away from something, yet he repetitively and compulsively returns to the "something" he is running away from.

Lauren Elkin's *Flâneuse: Women Walk the City in Paris, New York, Tokyo, Venice and London* puts up a solid case against the masculine monopoly of the cultural practice of flânerie.[10] The book is playfully subversive in terms of its content and style. It is like a walking tour through the literary and cultural history, biography, literary criticism and so on, challenging male dominance on the streets of history. The aim of the project of Elkin's detour through history seems to be the excavation and reconstruction of culturally and ideologically male-dominated historical sites to establish that the flâneuse was as much a presence on the streets as the *flâneur*.

Rosanne Kennedy proposes to read *The Rings of Saturn* by W. G. Sebald as a posthuman work. Critical of anthropocentric roots of the humanistic tradition, posthumanism invites humanities scholars to rethink the place of human beings in relation to non-human others, and ultimately to the planet and to the planet's future. Kennedy proposes that the literature of memoir and walking as practice contains the seeds of an alternative recognition of human beings as not autonomous but embedded in the natural and physical world. Instead of focussing exclusively on the human subject as in autobiography/biography, Sebald's walking memoirs portray the human as dependent on other species and on the natural world around.

Eluned Summers-Bremner reads Sebald's works in the light of Freudian – Lacanian theories of Psychoanalysis. She says that both Lacan and Sebald are concerned with the same subject matter: human suffering in the form of trauma, which is inexpressible in

---

10 Flânerie is a gender-neutral verb, which designates the practice of wandering in the city by both the sexes. See. *Oxford Dictionary of English*, Third Edition, 2010.

language. Sebald's literary works mourn a past traumatic event by creating an atmosphere that is neither past nor present. She refers to the Freudian-Lacanian premise that failure to mourn the loss of the love object leads to melancholia which might last until death. Trauma in Sebald, she observes, is "elaborated through the alterations and dislocations of readerly perspective performed by memory, visual and architectural technologies old and new, and walking."

The above works have, no doubt, brought out one or the other significant aspect of the experience of walking in their own ways, yet a comprehensive, systematic study, taking into account the various available writings, of walking as the object of literary creativity has not yet been undertaken. The present research project aims to break new ground in the direction of how human walking preferences have transformed since Rousseau's pioneering work, how walking came to be relegated in the modern age, and how it is re-emerging as a means to have a sense of the place in contemporary times.

Protesting against the Wheel: Walking as an Escape from Man/Machine Matrix

Walking has come a long way from being primarily a locomotive act ages ago to being a creative tool in the hands – or rather in the feet – of thinkers in an age dominated by automation. Walking, as practised by such persons, is actually a rediscovery of the physical act of walking to move from place A to B that has been performed half-consciously since the very beginning. It may be sometimes performed consciously as a subversive practice to pose a challenge to the onslaught of the wheel. The place in modern times has fragmented into a series of enclosed spaces – office, gym, mall, home, etc. – which have to be reached by the most efficient means of transportation. With walking having been displaced by faster means of transportation, humankind has once again been lifted out of their natural habitat as a dweller of the earth to live in artificially constructed spaces. Earlier, the hominids had left the forests for open space on earth;[11] now, people leave natural surroundings for artificially constructed spaces inside buildings or inside the cabins of moving vehicles where they are constrained to spend a considerable amount of time (Solnit). The change of habitat earlier had brought

---

11 See, *The Lost Art of Walking: The History, Science, Philosophy and Literature of Pedestrianism* by Geoff Nicholson, p. 8

them down on the earth from trees and had taught them how to walk (Amato 22). If the first change of habitat transformed humankind from arboreal species to walking and talking species, it would be worthwhile to study the transformations that the second, most significant shift has brought in the way humankind relates to its new habitat. Recent developments in social sciences have anticipated the effects of the environment on the human mind and behaviour; there is also a study, namely Psychogeography, by Guy Debord, to designate the effects of the geographical environment on the human mind and behaviour.[12] There has also been some speculation on the kinship between walking and writing: do both writing and walking mark the text and the space and attribute meaning to them in much the same way?[13] In *The Practice of Everyday Life*, Michel de Certeau writes, "The act of walking . . . is a process of appropriation of the topographical system on the part of the pedestrian; it is a special acting-out of the place . . . and it implies relations among differentiated positions" (97-98). If walking is one way of occupying and making sense of the world around, writing seems to be the other way of travelling in the mind and in the realm of abstract thought from one motif to another to arrive at a sense of it (Nicholson 27).

Modern life brought about a kind of thoughtless travel.[14] Moving around while tied immobilised on a seat in a plane, a boat, or a ship is travelling, not movement in the sense of using the body for locomotion. Contrary to "travelling," walking slows down the pace of movement of the body and puts it into its natural rhythm. Walking through a landscape with its scents, sights and sounds establishes a parallel "walk" in the abstract realm of thoughts, thus, establishing a sensuous connection with the place on which the mind can project its thought light to enlarge its horizons. This puts the

---

12 See *Psychogeography* by Merlin Coverley, Pocket Essentials Series.

13 See, for example, *The Art of Wandering: Writer as Walker* by Merlin Coverley and *Ways of Walking: Ethnography and Practice on Foot* edited by Tim Ingold and Jo Lee Vergunst.

14 Travelling on foot facilitates integration and communion with the surroundings. A traveller on foot has time to pay attention to the place to gather a sense of it. A lot of travel literature is about travellers' encounters with the locals who tell them hi (stories) about the place. Such hi (stories) impregnate the place with life and make it meaningful. Meeting with people and chance encounters with the wild animals is out of the question when one is travelling by car, an aeroplane, a ship etc.

internal and the external into consonance, triggering a thought process that is uniquely associated with and conditioned by landscape (Solnit 11-12).

Walking as movement on foot is different from travel as one can travel around the world yet not move at all. What the movement on foot can give, travelling in a vehicle cannot give at all. It is the body propelled locomotion and the sights, scents and scenes as well as people one meets on the way that makes the movement experientially special. Solnit says that walking becomes ambivalent and enormously creative in this way, and, in a sense, the walker arrives as soon as he takes the first step. Walking through sights and scenes allows the mind to connect the internal and abstract with the external and concrete, to join the unfamiliar with the new to form new thought compounds. Hence walking has been an indispensable activity for thinkers through the ages. And so, the history of walking is inextricably associated with the history of thinking and writing. It is precisely this relation between walking, thinking and writing that this research project proposes to investigate.

There are several contemporary eminent writers who foreground the practice of walking in quite avant-grade ways, such as Annie Dillard, Robert Macfarlane, Valeria Luiselli and W. G. Sebald. They evince no urge to conceal walking in their writing as something unworthy of mention. Rather, they not only practice it on the page of the text as a literary trope but also use it as a tool to achieve creative awareness, to visit the sites of their interest and to have a walker's look at the places. Therefore, in their works, the act of walking transcends mere physicality to become a literary, cultural and spiritual practice. Annie Dillard, for example, in *Pilgrim at the Tinker Creek,* urges the reader to wake up to the feel of nature and *see* it as Adam might have seen it when he first set his foot on earth. She says that to experience the divine, one does not have to walk but let the urge of walking overtake the body, mind and soul, and flow with the divine spirit. Robert Macfarlane explores the relationship between landscape and the human mind. Footpaths, he says, are ways of writing on the surface of the land. A landscape lined with footpaths is like a book; walkers experience the memories and the traces of the past walkers and leave their own footmarks to be re-treaded by successive generations of walkers. The need to understand our surroundings from a more subjective point of view is the central concern of Valeria Luiselli in *Sidewalks*. Her walking journey into the city is a simultaneous movement into her subjectivity, where objective sense impressions melt and fuse into new compounds. Much like W.G. Sebald, she interrogates monuments and city centres that shore up the modern edifice of abstraction, denying any play of subjectivity in the mind of the onlooker.

Since the diaries and memoirs written by these persons exemplify consistent co-occurrence of walking and thinking, there must be a relation between the two. Further, the behind-the-scenes act-of-walking in earlier writers has now come to the forefront in the texts of twentieth and twentieth first-century writers. This shows that the co-occurrence of walking and thinking has crystallised into a kind of steadfast companionship. The literature born out of this union may be termed as "the literature of walking," but it is yet to be recognised as a distinct genre of literature. Often categorised under titles such as "descriptive poetry," "nature poetry," or at best "travel literature," the literature of walking cannot be adequately described by these labels. To give the literature of walking its due place in literature, there is a need to study such writing on its own terms. Hence, our hypothesis that there is a distinct and significant sub-genre of nonfiction that deals primarily with walking and may, therefore, be described as the literature of walking, that its beginnings can be traced to Rousseau's *Reveries of the Solitary Walker* (1782), that a study of the literature of walking can reveal the changing engagement of the human being with the world, that this engagement has been a matter of critical and creative reflection, and finally that a study of this kind has the potential to disclose the modern subject's changing relationship with the world outside as well as within himself/herself.

Accordingly, the research problem has three levels: first is tracing the emergence of the modern subject as a "thinker on feet;" the second is finding the nature of the changing relationship of the walking and writing subject with the world and himself/herself, and the third is studying the various historically determined aspects of human experience captured by certain distinguished thinkers and writers whose writings are based chiefly on walking as a mode of transacting with the world.

Some of the texts proposed to be studied belong to the eighteenth and nineteenth century such as Jean-Jacques Rousseau's *Reveries of the Solitary Walker* (1782), Henry David Thoreau's *Walden, or, Life in the Woods* (1854) and "Walking" (1861), Charles Dickens' *The Uncommercial Traveller* (1860) and Charles Baudelaire's *The Painter of*

Modern Life (1863); along with some twentieth and twenty-first-century texts such as Loren Eiseley's *The Immense Journey* (1957), Anne Dillard's *Pilgrim at Tinker Creek* (1974), W. G. Sebald's *The Rings of Saturn* (1995), Robert Macfarlane's *The Old Ways: A Journey on Foot* (2012) and Valeria Luiselli's *Sidewalks* (2013).

Rousseau's *Reveries of the Solitary Walker* (1782) treats walking as a way to study the "self." Rejected by society, Rousseau walks to a self-imposed exile in the wilderness of nature. *Reveries* is a written record of his thoughts during that time. During moments of epiphany, he discovers that he himself has been his own enemy who was siding with society to torment his soul. He comes to the awareness that one has to know and narrate oneself to avoid being misunderstood and misrepresented by a society that judges to condemn. It is only when one accepts what society says what one is that one is most painfully alienated from oneself. Rousseau's *Reveries* demonstrates, in John Muir's words, that "going out" was really "going in" (427).

By saying that people around him were leading a life of "quiet desperation" (10), Henry David Thoreau in *Walden, or, Life in the Woods* (1854), heralded modernist critique long before it registered its formal arrival. With human beings no longer sojourners in nature, says Thoreau, a terrible stagnation and spiritual ennui has set in which has been widely accepted as human destiny. Prophetically, Thoreau states that "[m]en have become the tools of their tools" (33). He finds contemporary lifestyle no less than a new form of slavery as masses are compelled to work like bonded labourers for acquiring the things they do not actually need. Having lived an austere life for some time near Walden Pond, Thoreau observes that after working for about six weeks in a year, he could meet all the expenses for that year and had the rest of the time to himself (58). He talks about the mellifluous music of wind and birds, intoxicating sips of water of Walden Pond, absorbing and soul-refreshing walking trips in the woods. He avers that these things cannot be bought and sold, and those "superfluities" which are bought and sold in the market are not required for a really happy life. One has to prune one's life to the very basics to enjoy living.

Thoreau says that most of us sleepwalk through life; hence, nothing new can ever happen unless we "wake up." He urges humankind to consider its true spiritual moorings in these words: "[I]f we are really dying, let us hear the rattle in our throats and feel cold in the extremities; if we are alive, let us go about our business"

(81). Being a philosopher of freedom, he values the non-committal and vita contemplativa[15] way of living above all.

Thoreau begins his essay "Walking" by contrasting the "absolute freedom and wildness" in nature with the heavily compromised freedom in society. He considers walking as art that few understand, let alone practise. For him, it is an opportunity to be a part of nature. Derived from "à la Sainte Terre," a wanderer sans any territory, a "saunterer" is he who has no home of his own but is at home everywhere. Thoreau prefers the kind of walking that is more like a crusade. He hints that walking is a kind of meditation that wins the territory of "self" from the demons of modern life and frees the mind from the ligatures that fix it to mundane realities; it lifts it high to contemplate philosophical, sublime and divine truth. For such meditative walking, one has to free oneself from all bonds.

The third work in the list, namely *The Uncommercial Traveller*, is a series of sketches written by Dickens for his weekly magazine *All the Year Round* in the 1860s. In it, Dickens has combined the abstract motif of life as travel, during which the traveller leaves his memories and traces behind to be read by those who come following his footsteps, with the physical act of travelling/walking to a destination and meeting people and seeing places on the way. It is a record of the narrator's – who is a disguised voice of the author himself – travels/walks around a number of locations such as workhouses, theatres and churches, factories and alms-houses. Besides London, the "uncommercial traveller" visits Liverpool twice to have a look at the docks; he travels to the city of Rochester where he had spent his childhood, to the dockyard at Chatham, to Italy and twice to France where he visits a mortuary. The essays document the Victorian way of social observation and articulation (Chris R. 523).

Charles Baudelaire in *The Painter of Modern Life* (1964) says that an artist has to be a man of the crowd; he cannot just suffice to be a being who keeps to himself in the ivory tower, rather he has to come down to be with people. Referring to an artist M. G., Baudelaire goes on to say that he loves to walk/travel around incognito, i.e. he holds his identity in suspended animation just to be able to mingle completely with the crowd. What Baudelaire further emphasises is that the beauty that the artist is after is made up of twin elements: the

15 The term denoting a life of contemplation has been coined by Hannah Arendt in her book *Human Condition*, 1958, Chicago University Press.

enduring universal and the fleeting present. It is through the portrayal of the fleeting present that the artist strives to offer a glimpse of the eternal to the reader/spectator.

"Seeing," as Loren Eiseley practices in *The Immense Journey* (1957), is not the "seeing" of a naturalist alone but also that of an imaginative philosopher who walks in order to have a fresh look at things, especially the fossilised remains. He sees through them and beyond them simultaneously. "The Slit," the first section of the book, is a metaphor for a special kind seeing-up closely and seeing through the skull of a creature that Eiseley finds in a pit. The sight of the skull inspires Eiseley to utter a monologue reimagining the skull into life and the possible connection of human beings with it. He does not so much focus on it as an object as he treats it as a window to the evolutionary secrets of mammals. Eiseley tries to find traces of the unknown journey of human beings down the ages in the natural world around him in the form of fossils. The range of his studies is so diverse as to include primates, prairie dogs, the ocean depths, the progress of "the snout," flowers and plants, birds, the development of the human brain, and even robots.

Eiseley's wonder at the sudden emergence of human beings on earth as the predominant species seems to be the motivating force behind his lifelong passion for studying the evolutionary process. However, unlike Darwin, Eiseley puts forward an anti-teleological view of human evolution. He aptly observes that our worldview is still essentially Ptolemaic, i.e. human-centred; and he urges readers not to look for a purpose in the long evolutionary journey of human beings, and also, not to commit the mistake that "life is now adjusted for eternity…" (Eiseley 14).

Annie Dillard's *Pilgrim at Tinker Creek* (1974) is based on her experiments with seeing during her walks around a creek near her lodging. Her seeing is not just seeing the objects around her but also includes her being seen by them. Hers is a spiritual conception of the universe, with a sense of the presence of enormous power that flows on always but comes to be seen/felt unbidden in some unselfconscious moments. The very first image the book opens with holds the key to it. It urges the reader to wake up while doubting if the reader would ever wake up. When one actually wakes up, it feels like one has just set one's foot for the first time on earth. *Pilgrim at Tinker Creek* is an account of the narrator waking up to her surroundings. One has to *see* if one wants to enjoy the gifts of nature scattered all around. She quotes Stewart Edward White, who says that one has to forget the "naturally obvious" and construct the "artificial obvious" to experience the real (20). For seeing, one has to walk in nature because it is the only way to approach nature respectfully; and it is to the walker that nature opens up her secrets. Human beings have been gifted with a secret network of ganglia which, without our knowledge, edits everything that goes to the brain; only unicellular creatures can experience the universe as it is because they do not have this editing mechanism in them. What that pure seeing could be like, Dillard comes to find in the testimonies of newly-sighted people who do not perceive the world as anything more than empty colour patches unencumbered by meaning. It is this pure, innocent experience of seeing that she longs to have in her life. In one of such encounters, she comes to know that seeing is letting yourself flow unselfconsciously in the flow of the universal spirit so that you not only see but also are seen by that powerful presence. While trying to do this, one is always pulled down by the "useless interior babble" (34); one has to raise one's sights above this "muddy river" to peep into the "realm of the real where subjects and objects act and rest purely" (34).

In *The Old Ways: A Journey on Foot* (2012), Robert Macfarlane explores the relationship between landscape and the human mind. Footpaths, he says, are ways of writing on the surface of the land. A landscape webbed with footpaths is as good as a book; it is writeable as well as readable. This process of writing and reading is simultaneous; a generation of walkers leaves its footprints to be read/followed by the next generation even as it too reads the footprints of previous generations. This way, the footpaths accumulate corpora of stories, narratives, experiences, legends, memory maps in the shared memory of people associated with them. Interestingly, a significant number of words about thinking and learning have their origins in human interaction with land. For example, Macfarlane discovers that the verbs "to learn" and "to write" have come from the felt human experience with the land; at one point in the history of language, "to write," meant track making and "to learn," meant finding a path (105). He supports his claims with extensive research in the works of both ancient and modern authors, coupled with his own first-hand experience of walking in distant lands.

W. G. Sebald in his *The Rings of Saturn* (1995) brings to bear an encyclopaedic knowledge with so epic a sweep of time and space on his vision that like the mythological Tiresias his eye can scan the past, present and future at once. The very first episode – when the narrator is lying supine, half-conscious on a hospital bed, desiring a look at "reality" but finds an "insensate spot" (4) in the black netted window of the hospital room – hints at the kind of situation the modern human being has got himself in. S/he is incarcerated in a heavily fortified structure, again a metaphor of paraphernalia of modernity, which impedes a direct contact with reality; it affords only a distant, dim and highly compromised peep at reality. This image is followed by a ghoulish scene of the dissection of a cadaver by a guild of surgeons. This image is a powerful metaphor striking at the roots of Cartesian philosophy, which overlooks human flesh to attend to the so-called machine within. Then, alluding to Thomas Browne, the narrator remarks that the fog that rises from a body opened soon after death engulfs one's mind for life. Following these two episodes is a trail of unrelenting and all-pervasive destruction wrought by "befogged" minds threatening the very future of humankind.

Valeria Luiselli, in her book *Sidewalks* (2013), suggests that modern ignorance of the need to understand our surroundings from a more subjective point of view is leading to a kind of crisis in our lives. To have a more personal approach to the outside world, she tries to read the city like a book and to write the book like a stroll on the sidewalks in a city. Much like W.G. Sebald, she interrogates modern monuments and city centres. She questions modern abstraction and the simulated world and bemoans the passive acceptance of these reductive representations with no urge on our part to have a look at the concrete and the real. She questions the tendency for reductive representation of complex phenomena by interrogating the disciplines of cartography and anatomy. She seems to challenge relational thinking as the basis of modern rationality, which, for the sake of simplicity, has substituted the imagined abstract for the felt real. As a result, this convenient substitution has gone on to engulf the real so that it is on the verge of being lost altogether. For Luiselli, even walking, the cherished pastime of thinkers to have a sense of the world, has lost its pristine appeal for us. The city decides the route, rhythm and pace of the urban walker. Any modulation in the set patterns may invite the risk of being either knocked down by buzzing traffic or treated as an object of suspicion by the city police.

Thus, inspired by the walking writers, the project unfolds in the form of wandering pathways of thought that criss-cross each other on the landscape of the mind in the same way as "...the act of walking provokes and engenders the act of writing" (Coverley 13-14).

CHAPTER 1

Walking to Study the Self: Jean Jacques Rousseau's *Reveries of the Solitary Walker*

> Philosophers walked. But philosophers who thought about walking are rarer.
>
> (Solnit)
>
> I can only meditate when I am walking when I stop I cease to think; my mind only works with my legs.
>
> *Confessions*, Rousseau 382)
>
> We should really see our shadow, instead of mindlessly living it out.
>
> (*Myth*, Jung 167)
>
> The récit de voyage effects and demonstrates this double journey that is all reading; it can carry the perpendicular path along with it to effect a displacement of the reader, to change his mental location, and finally, it can change his physical location. ("Travel and Writing," Butor 4)

If time be a straight horizontal line with the past and the future meeting at the centre (Thoreau, *Walden* 19), the point of origin of both the timelines; and the vertical line of space intersect the line of time at the centre, then moving along the line of time amounts to a parallel movement along the line of space as well. In our world, there come from time to time travellers from the past and from the future to dwell in the present. These human beings are so preoccupied with *their* (emphasis added) time zones that they feel "out of time" in the present. In order to connect with and live "their past" or "their future," they like to travel mostly along the spatial axis. There is a long history of such saints, thinkers, philosophers and writers of genius who preferred walking to any other mode of travelling. However, as an exception, some people can travel along the time axis sitting at one place, i.e. without physically moving an inch on the land (Thoreau, "Walking"). By virtue of their profound connection with the past and the future, they offer insights to improve the present, they sensitise humankind to their follies, they show the way out of hopelessness and utter prophecies about the future. Jean Jacques Rousseau and Henry David Thoreau are two such travellers from distant time zones: Rousseau was too futuristic to be comfortable in his contemporary world, and Thoreau was too much preoccupied with the past (for the better of humankind) that he had to retreat to the woods to "live" in it. Rousseau antagonised many by his candid attitude in his writings towards the ills of his society and had to spend most of his life in exile ("Introduction," France). Thomas Bentley, an Englishman who visited him in the summer of 1776, writes that Rousseau belongs not in the world but in the region above it.

> He is a musical instrument above the concert pitch, and therefore too elevated for the present state of society, and all his singularities and errors, as they are called, proceed from the extreme delicacy of his sensations. I was so taken up with his intellect that I have almost forgot how it was clothed, though I remember he has small slender body, rather below the common size, that he has a thin palish face with delicate features, and that he has a great deal of expression in his eyes and a countenance when he is either pleased or displeased, one of which he certainly is every moment, for nothing that he sees or hears or thinks of is indifferent to him. When Nature was making this singular being, one would imagine she intended him for an inhabitant of the air, but before she had finished his wings he eagerly sprung out of her hands, and his unfinished body sunk him down to the earth. (Bentley qtd. in France)

Rousseau's *Reveries of the Solitary Walker* (1782) is a work strikingly different from his earlier works in the sense that it deals not with the questions of philosophy, ethics, morality, society, education, etc., but with the "man himself and all his contradictions" (France). For fifteen years before 1776, when he began writing *Reveries*, Rousseau suffered terribly at the hands of a belligerent society ("First Walk" Rousseau). By walking and self-contemplating in the company of nature, he is able to regain sanity, the experience of which he shares with the readers in his last work, *Reveries*. Moreover, *Reveries* is a recollection of his past life, in which Rousseau applied certain philosophical ideas to his life. At his old age, he wants to have a re-look at his past actions by recreating them while walking and thinking. He wants to arrange his life experiences into a logical account to be offered to God after death.

Reveries is a foundational work in the literature of walking. The literature of walking is a term used for literature depicting a walker thinking about himself vis-à-vis the surroundings. The literature of walking does not describe an idea, theme, or phase in history; it spells out the play of the mind. The "river of consciousness" is captured by walking at its literal and literary background. It is true of all the literature of walking that it defies the traditional straightjacket of genre and neat, logical and linear cohesion. It is the flow that is important, not the focus. This cannot be more at display anywhere than in Rousseau's *Reveries*. It is noteworthy that Rousseau is the pioneer of foregrounding the practice of walking in his writings. In his *Reveries,* each chapter is a walk. Not that earlier writers did not practise walking, but they usually kept it behind the literary curtains. Rousseau had made the practice of walking no less than a character in his *Reveries*. Feeling rejected by society, Rousseau walks to a self-imposed exile in the wilderness of nature. Rousseau practises solitary walking to heal his anguished self, and *Reveries* is a written record of his thoughts during that time. During moments of epiphany, he discovers himself to be his enemy, who was siding with society to torment his soul. By slow degrees, he comes to an awareness that one has to know and narrate oneself to avoid being described by a society that judges to condemn. It is only when one accepts what society says what one is, that one is most painfully alienated from oneself. Rousseau's *Reveries* shows, in John Muir's words, that "going out" was really "going in" (427).

Comprising "Ten Walks," *Reveries* is Rousseau's last piece of writing. After his death in July 1778, the working manuscript of *Reveries* was retrieved from his belongings. As the last work, *Reveries* present a "faithful" record of Rousseau's walking reflections. Each chapter is composed like a stroll with a reverie on an idea or memory recalled from his past. They are the last walks of a man "alone on earth" (Rousseau "First Walk"), in which, he says, he would apply "the barometer to his soul" ("First Walk"). The last walk is fragmentary, a walk into infinity from which he never returns.

Long walks in nature help Rousseau recall memories of the past trauma repressed in the unconscious. Then he thinks about them afresh and strives to redress the old wounds on his psyche. During the prolonged walking and thinking sessions, Rousseau summons memories of the past from their dark resting place and makes them appear before the conscious mind as if they are visitors from the past. Rousseau uses walking alone as a tool to talk to his troubled self. While walking, Rousseau is able to read out from his soul aloud. In this way, Rousseau uses walking as a tool for "acting out his intimate self" (Bradshaw 206), a kind of walking meditation to heal the wounded psyche. Nature, for Rousseau, is not an objective reality. Rather it is, as Burt suggests, allegorical spreading out of his intimate self (233), to be recollected and reclaimed after thorough re-examination. Rousseau's walking and thinking amid nature can thus be seen as "a pretext for the encounter of self with himself in a natural setting" (Burt 232). Paul de Man also agrees, saying that the external and internal reality act as mirrors to one another. To quote, "The sensory manifestation of art and literature is the outside of an inner content which is itself an outer event or entity that has been internalised" (Man 771). Lane regards Rousseau's *Reveries* as forming part of nature writing in which an author experiences a "blissful loss of consciousness of self" (474) into the "all-encompassing whole" (474). To be more precise, argues Lane, such writings can be termed as "convergence" writings as the individual, and the cosmic self merge into one another. But Lane's argument overlooks the primary act of walking as the catalyst to set this process in motion, and by being in the background, provides the right environment for the marriage of the individual and the cosmic self, the experience of which Rousseau aptly terms as a "reverie."

All of Rousseau's walks, except the last one, follow a cyclical pattern of repetition and recollection. At the outset of each walk, he rues he has been wronged unjustly by society, that he loves everyone, but they, on the contrary, have fixed their happiness on his pain, that he has been forced to live the life of a solitary man despite his being most sociable of all. This runs like the refrain of a trauma narrative throughout the nine walks. However, this thought returns with lesser and lesser intensity in each successive walk. When he walks for some distance with these thoughts in his mind, he is slowly able to set his mind free from their hold. Then, by slow degrees, he begins to notice the panorama of nature. His senses, which were earlier turned inwards and preoccupied with painful memories, open out to register the sights and sounds of nature, and he finds himself temporarily free from the rumblings of "unassimilated trauma" (Lacan 55) lying deep in the unconscious.

Freud spoke of trauma as something irreconcilable with the existing set of defence mechanisms (24). He further states that the trauma that lies beyond the symbolic keeps on destabilising the symbolic order. So long as the subject is not able to express the trauma in the language of the symbolic, it continues to have hysterical symptoms, the intensity of which varies from case to case and person-to-person (27). According to his insights, the account of the occurrence of trauma given by the subject in such a state is hardly reliable; it is only an externally visible bulge or warp caused by the real manifesting itself in the form of trauma from behind the scene. Since real, because of its nature, is "inassimilable" and beyond the symbolic order (as Lacan views it), it is not to be expressed in the language/narrative – which acts like a smoke screen covering it – of trauma. Trauma is further defined as a "situation of dissociation or "absence" from the self, in which, the victim unconsciously imitate[s], or identifie[s] with the aggressor or traumatic scene" (Leys 8). As an experience of "hypnotic imitation or identification" with the aggressor/seducer (9), trauma has a devastating effect on the subject's "cognitive-perceptual capacities" (9). In his initial version of trauma studies, Freud had suggested that "a precocious experience of sexual relations...resulting from sexual abuse committed by another person" (Ringel 2) might cause hysterical symptoms later on in the personality of a victim adult. Later, he built upon this "seduction theory" to expound "conflict theory," which held that it is not the memory of external trauma but the "unacceptable nature of sexual and aggressive wishes" (2) that caused hysterical symptoms. However, sexuality remains fundamental to both the theories. As mentioned earlier, the concept of trauma as given by Sigmund Freud and Jacques Lacan is essential to understanding Rousseau's *Reveries*.

Jacques Lacan remarks trauma is the "kernel of the real" (53) that forms the basis of one's personality. Therefore, I can argue that Rousseau's self-pitying complaints of being unjustly wronged are workings of "phantasy" (Lacan 60) aimed at coming to terms with something "quite primary" (60) lying at the core. "The place of the real," to quote Lacan, "… stretches from the trauma to the phantasy – in so far as the phantasy is never anything more than the screen that conceals something quite primary ..." (60). Using these psychological insights to understand the confessions in *Reveries*, one can hope to find answers to some of the nagging questions. What forced Rousseau to undertake self-examination? What is the root cause of Rousseau's terrible maladjustments in society? What is the reason behind his sweeping condemnation of one and all as not worthy people? What is it he expects from friends and acquaintances? Are those expectations justified from ordinary people? In a nutshell, who is he still looking for in every individual (especially the "innocent girls") he comes in contact with? And finally, how does walking become a transformative act in the entire process?

The answer to these questions lies in the "Tenth Walk," where Rousseau admits he had had a premature sexual initiation by a much older woman and that experience went on to decide his fate for the rest of his life. This experience was remarkable because the relationship was fraught with mother/mistress ambivalence. The woman in question was twelve years senior, and he used to call her "Mamma" ("Tenth Walk"). The very nature of the relationship sealed the impossibility of its repetition, and with it, the impossibility of Rousseau's ever coming to terms with it in his subsequent life. It is the memory of the trauma of premature contact and separation from this woman that lies at the core of Rousseau's personality. And the role of psychoanalysis is to "isolate in the subject a kernel" (Lacan 250) of the real – which might manifest as trauma (55) – of his personality, and bring it up to the realm of the symbolic for accepting, narrating and integrating it in the subject's personality. This is what Rousseau has attempted and succeeded in doing with himself, which can be termed as self-psychoanalysis. It is during walking that he is able to conjure up the buried traumatic past to the consciousness for a close examination. To do that, Rousseau splits his mind into two – the analyst and the patient. What Rousseau has done with himself can be termed as a "walking cure" instead of the Freudian "talking cure."

Walking – if correctly practised – can become an act, a rhythm and an anodyne, letting the walker submerge in the deep realms of the mind and talk to his troubled soul. With Rousseau, walking assumes the significance of a redemptive pilgrimage to the depths of the self. In this respect, Rousseau is the first person in the literature of walking who took ten walking pilgrimages down the recesses of the self. Had it not been for his unwavering and Oedipus-like determination to find the perpetrators of the crime, he would have retracted after the very first walk. But he walked longer and longer to go deeper and deeper into the mind. At last, he reaches from where he never returns.

Each of Rousseau's walks tests an abstract idea on the touchstone of the experience of his life, which leads to surprising findings. In the "First Walk," Rousseau spells out the plan to walk and think about the self; in the "Second Walk," Rousseau muses on the "memory" of his past life; in the "Third Walk," he probes "learning;"

in the "Fourth Walk," he studies the theory and practice of "truth;" in the "Sixth Walk," he reflects on the concept and experience of "happiness;" in the "Seventh Walk," he rediscovers his love of walking and botanising; in the "Eighth Walk" and "Ninth Walk" he returns to the idea of happiness; in the "Tenth Walk," he feels happy and completely free from pain.

In the "First Walk," Rousseau refers to Montaigne, the French essayist, like whose *Essais* his *Reveries* would portray the intimate "self" of the author. "I describe not the essence but the passage," wrote Montaigne (qtd. in Rousseau), and Rousseau's title too hints at something as fluid and changing as the stream of thoughts in a wandering mind. Rousseau himself says, "My whole life has been little else than a long reverie divided into chapters by my daily walks" (France). Also, in the "First Walk," he says that he aims to examine his soul and report what he would find there, like "a series of barometer readings" ("First Walk"). However, there is a method behind the apparent veil of spontaneity and aimlessness of *Reveries*. Therefore, *Reveries* hardly seem to be the loose thoughts of a vagabond in distress. Rousseau states the aim of undertaking the walks.

> So now I am alone in the world, with no brother, neighbour or friend, nor any company left me but my own. The most sociable and loving of men has with one accord been cast out by all the rest….*what am I* (emphasis mine)? This must now be the object of my inquiry. ("First Walk")

Rousseau is practising solitary walking in the company of nature. The solitude of Rousseau is of a different kind; he is alone and not alone at the same time. While he says that he is dejected at being rejected by some kinds of company that humans keep, such as brother, neighbour, friend; he keeps the company of his own self ("First Walk"). Having his own company means for him he has a store of memories of the people vis-à-vis himself. When he explores the self in solitude, he finds it like a theatre vibrant with all sorts of characters who had affected him in some way in the past. It is there that he would re-rehearse and relive his role vis-à-vis theirs. In this case, he has the busiest company ever. He is sociable because even in solitude, he loves, tends and cares not only about his friends but about their memories as well, and dearest to him of all are those who chose to be openly vitriolic without hiding their anger under a mask ("First Walk"). As Michael Davis observes, Rousseau's "I" is in an objective case, which means that he is looking at himself as if he were an "object" of his enquiry (94-95).

Rousseau feels that he has been so overwhelmed by the collective scorn and hatred of his tormentors that he has not been able to cope with it, and that it has lain stuck in this heart for a long time. Time and again, he finds himself dreaming as if he is still in the midst of people who cast aspersions on him. At times, he feels as if he is going mad. With vicious propaganda, reflects Rousseau, they have presented him in such a bad light that he gets scared of his depictions. With weapons of hate and propaganda, muses Rousseau, his detractors, wanted to control his destiny, and they have been successful for ten long years. For some time, Rousseau seeks to resist this onslaught, but this leads to more self-torment. At last, he gains freedom by submitting to the inevitable. Yet, he tries to clutch at the last hope of redeeming his image in the eyes of posterity, but he fears even that might not be possible. With this utterly resigned state of mind about the torments of the present and being stoically unsure of the future, Rousseau recollects the memories of his past. With the act of walking through the landscape, he endeavours to register the perambulations of his mind. He says that his excessive suffering has become its own anodyne and immunised him from further pain.

> Everything is finished for me on this earth. Neither good nor evil can be done to me by any man. I have nothing left in the world to fear or hope for, and this leaves me in peace at the bottom of the abyss, a poor unfortunate mortal, but as unmoved as God himself. ("First Walk")

In the last days of his life, muses Rousseau, he would turn his senses inwards to examine the memories in his mind to prepare the account that he will have to offer to God after death. However, Rousseau feels that since he has been cleansed of all passion "in the crucible of adversity" ("First Walk"), he may not find any residue of resentment towards his former tormentors. Now that he is feeling detached from his body and his senses are dimming, the flowering of the soul has come as a surprise to him. He finds this transformation strange and worth examining. Moreover, three-hour walking every day fills his soul with ecstasy, which makes him regret why he did not begin walking earlier when he was suffering terribly. Thus, he resolves to study his soul and make a record of the findings so gathered. Since he has regained sanity after a long spell of suffering, he wants to store the present delightful state of mind in the form of "reveries" so that in the last years of his life he can feel the same joy by reading them.

Michel Butor expresses the similar view that reading a travel account may recall the actual travel undertaken when the work was being written; therefore, it can offer an escape from the present time into that distant past captured in the text as word images. He writes in "Travel and Writing" that if we examine the body language of people returning from their daylong work at a metro station during the evening rush hour, we will find that their excessive boredom is being expressed through physical "symptoms" like moving their eyes aimlessly from one object to another, fiddling with some trivial object, staring blankly at some mundane object and so on. Exemplifying the power of reading travel literature (written by oneself or somebody else) as a form of escape from the boring/painful present, he further notes that there is a possibility that one may find in the midst of bored out people someone absorbed in reading a book with his eyes fixed on the words on the page to the point of being lost in the world of the book. To quote, "[h]is eyes never leave the volume he fingers slowly, running along the line after line, penetrating page after page. He smiles, beams in expectation. *He has found an outlet, he is elsewhere* (emphasis added): in the London fog, on the mesas of the Wild West, searching medieval forests, or even in the soundproofed room, the laboratory of the "writer" (2). Michel Butor, however, ignored the role of walking in thinking and writing – for Butor, any form of travelling is as good as walking. However, walking and thinking are inextricably connected in Rousseau's *Reveries*.

Similarly, in the "Second Walk," Rousseau clings to the hope that reading his *Reveries* in his old age, he would recollect the memories of the past when he used to practise the art of walking and thinking because being old, he would not be able to experience the world as passionately as he used to when he was young. To quote Butor again, "[t]he escape which it [reading] provides from the wounding, pressing, the hateful, obscure daily world makes reading a ceremony of purification, a ceremony often reinforced by a complete ritual" (3). Intriguingly, by walking and thinking at present, Rousseau recollects the happy, youthful experiences of his past, which would serve as an anodyne for his expected pains and loneliness at the time of his death in the future. Thus, *Reveries* is also a recollection of the walking and introspection practised many years back.

> … if I am to contemplate myself before my decline, I must go back several years to the time when, losing all hope for this life and finding no food left on earth for my soul, I gradually learnt to feed it on its own substance and seek all its nourishment within myself. ("Second Walk")

Rousseau states he experienced self-sufficiency while walking and meditating on the self. The only way to re-experience the past, says Rousseau, is by reliving the memories in our minds. Rousseau finds walking helpful in recalling memories of consciousness. Rousseau repents he is undertaking his walking meditation too late in his life when his creative and imaginative faculties have undergone much decline. Yet, he resolves firmly to carry out this task of self-examination before leaving this world.

> These hours of solitude and meditation are the only ones in the day when I am completely myself and my own master, with nothing to distract or hinder me, the only ones when I can truly say that I am what nature meant me to be. ("Second Walk")

It is in the state of consciousness that one attains the ability to access the inaccessible, filter the unfiltered, arrange the deranged and untangle the entangled layers of the sedimented experiences lying asleep in the unconscious. Rousseau, with this ability at his command, finds himself immune to all the pains that society inflicts on him. Even the bitterest memories of his life cannot stop him from enjoying the ecstasies of the soul. In this neutral state of mind, he even thanks his persecutors without whose slander and scorn he could never have attained to this high level of awareness. Rousseau says that walking led to the discovery of treasures that lay within him and he would routinely make use of these treasures lest he should forget that he has them. Later on in this walk, Rousseau describes an accident in which he, after being hit by an onrushing Great Dane, fell on the ground badly injured. Because of the impact, he suffered brief amnesia. The description of the effects of the accident on Rousseau's mind runs like an allegory:

> I was conscious of nothing else. In this instant I was being born again, and it seemed as if all I perceived was filled with my frail existence. Entirely taken up by the present, I could remember nothing; I had no distinct notion of myself as a person, nor had I the least idea of what had just happened to me. I did not know who I was, nor where I was; I felt neither pain, fear, nor anxiety…. They asked me where I lived; I was unable to answer. I asked them where I was; they said 'at the Upper Milepost,' but they might as well have said 'at Mount Atlas.' I had to ask in turn the name of the country, the town and the district where I was. Even this was not enough, it took me the whole way from there to the Boulevard to remember my address and my name. ("Second Walk")

Rousseau explains that the pain caused by the accident was more of psychological nature than merely physical. He states that even after the accident, he could walk a mile to reach his home. But it was quite some time before he could recall his name and home address – so profound was its effect on his memory. Thus, the accident was more a blow to his mind than to his body. The months after the accident brought a series of scandalous rumours about him, which caused even more mental agony. In one such incident, a lady falsely attributed a scandalous statement in her novel to Rousseau, in which she criticised monarchs for not looking after their people's welfare. In another such rumour, Rousseau was presumed dead from the recent accident. Even his obituary appeared in a magazine. Rousseau also heard that some people were working to attribute some scandalous writings to his name after his death. Happening of so many chance incidents, soon after the accident, detrimental to his peace of mind and reputation, made Rousseau believe that he was under a "universal conspiracy" ("Second Walk") and all his enemies are supported by the cruel fate to inflict torments on him. These traumatic events so affected Rousseau's mind that he became stoically resigned to his fate.

One can read the accident involving Rousseau and the Great Dane as an allegory on his "self." During this accident, Rousseau suffered temporary amnesia, as he could not recall his name and whereabouts – people around him were trying to guess who he was. The incident allegorises that the social self of Rousseau was being described by others, as Rousseau could no longer tell about himself. Because of this accident, he suffered a break from his "real self" and internalised the self which was constructed by society. After the accident, Rousseau experiences his transformed reality as the "new normal" of his life. He begins to see himself and his world through the eyes of society, acting as the "other" in his personality. It is the internalisation of the "other" that led to his alienation from his self which he tries to recover in his subsequent walks. The physical fall heralds an overall decline in his faculties, fortunes, his social and financial status, and his reputation. E. S. Burt also remarks that Rousseau's texts are allegories (246). The cuts, bruises, injuries and sprains symbolise subsequent slanders on his character and reputation. Rousseau feels it is a divine decree that he should suffer. Therefore, accepting the will of God, he decides he would suffer without complaining.

> God is just; his will is that I should suffer, and he knows my innocence. That is what gives me confidence. My heart and my reason cry out that I shall not be disappointed. Let men and fate do their worst, we must learn to suffer in silence, everything will find its proper place in the end and sooner or later my turn will come. ("Second Walk")

The "Third Walk" reminisces about the time of his life when he resolved to dedicate his life to learning. It begins with an epigraph from Solon, "Growing older, I learn all the time." At old age, Rousseau's experience stands in sharp contrast to the idea in the epigraph. From the experience of a lifetime, Rousseau concludes that the experience could have been worth having if he had gained it before the onset of adverse circumstances. He laments that knowledge about the behaviour of people gained from a bitter experience has never saved him from like experiences in the future. Rousseau believes that knowledge gathered from experience is not worth having if it comes too late in life to be put into practice with profit. For example, Rousseau trusted people who apparently liked him, or so he believed, but they eventually proved to be his worst enemies. His experience of having deceived once did not save him from more such traps in the future because every new friend approached him with a novel method to dupe him. Near the end of his life, he learns that the best way to deal with such people is to avoid them. But he regrets he does not have many years to live in which he can practise his dearly earned wisdom. He muses: "If an old man has something to learn, it is the art of dying" ("Third Walk"). Would he not have been better if they had spared him of the agony after which he became wise? Asks Rousseau. Even more so when this wisdom cannot help him avoid such people in future? Even if, says Rousseau, he learns to make use of his painfully earned knowledge to live better, he does not have many more years to live. "No doubt adversity is a brilliant teacher, but its lessons are dearly bought, and often the profit we gain from them is not worth the price they cost us" ("Third Walk"). Every time Rousseau walks to seek pleasure, he experiences pain first. Plato's observation that since the contraries owe their existence to one another and the experience of pain is a must for the sensation of pleasure (Brann 7) seems to be true with Rousseau.

Torn between the contrary impulses, Rousseau feels that given his sensitivity and urge to be always morally upright, he is a misfit in the world peopled by imperfect human beings. "I learned from early experience that I was not made for this world and that in it I would never attain the state to which my heart aspired" ("Second Walk"). Since he cannot control the cruel workings of fate against him, he poignantly concludes that resignation to suffering is the only option left to him. In this state of mind, he turns his mind inwards with the determination to find out "the nature and purpose of [his] being" ("Second Walk"). Comparing himself with other intellectuals, Rousseau dwells upon the notion of knowledge as embodied in and experienced by oneself, as against knowledge as an intellectual and abstract concept. During the same time, Rousseau has been a part of the group of philosophers called philosophes, who, unlike ancient philosophers, used philosophy not as a way of life but as a tool kit to solve their problems. They were not so much interested in philosophy for the betterment of self as to convince others (Gourevitch 495). Rousseau notes that there are people who have gained so deep an understanding of certain philosophies that they can discuss and debate, compare and contrast each school of philosophy, weigh and consider their merits and demerits, yet the knowledge, despite being so thoroughly mastered, remains external to them – only a memory stored in the mind that can be recalled on need to use basis. It is never assimilated into their being; it never reaches their soul and breathes the breath of life, and, therefore, it is never reflected in their actions and never becomes the guiding force in their way of living.

Rousseau's idea of philosophy is practical, the philosophy that emerges out of one's experience, the philosophy that has been tested on the touchstone of conscience, the philosophy that informs one's actions and daily conduct, the philosophy that is based on the highest ethos of morality, the philosophy for which one is prepared to live and die like Socrates, the philosophy that is not for instructing others but for oneself, the philosophy that is not a mask on a selfish hidden doctrine of self-promotion. According to Rousseau, such a philosophy is not worth having.

Rousseau feels that his ideas are based on transcendental truths that his detractors cannot understand. How can he teach his experiential wisdom to the people the awareness of whom is limited to the senses? He admits he cannot offer logical rebuttals to the sophistry of his critics – "[his] heart answered them better than [his] reason" ("Third Walk") – yet he cannot shake off the painful memory of their maliciousness towards him. His traumatic experiences like Freud's notion of "the uncanny"[16] (219) rise and threaten the existence of his "ego," the peaceful equilibrium of opposing forces in the mind. Since it happens with traumatised people, the traumatic experiences rise and pose a threat to the sanity of the subject. It repeatedly rises with renewed intensity until it is "talked to" and resolved. Given his over-sensitivity to hurts, Rousseau has an accumulated "debt" of traumatic experiences; the memory of the same rises and falls – so does his consciousness. To have a re-look at his past requires that Rousseau should practise walking and thinking in a peaceful and solitary place. Rousseau believes that by confining him to solitary life "they [his critics] had done more for my happiness than I had been able to do myself" ("Second Walk"). With this statement, all his previous remarks regarding ostracism and learning stand drastically qualified. In other words, he now significantly alters his earlier views about being ostracised and this being the greatest agony of his life, as well as his previous view of Solon's remark, that he might have been better without having to learn the bitter lessons from the past.

In the "Fourth Walk," Rousseau recollects that phase of his life when he had resolved to live his life as per the motto of truthfulness. During the same time, Rousseau was also writing *Confessions* (1781). An accidental finding of old pamphlets prompted the memory of this phase of life. One day, he was reading the essay *Moralia* ("How a Man May Profit by His Enemies") by Plutarch. And, also, he found Juvenal's words – "vitam impendere vero" – on the title page of a Journal by Abbé Rozier. Rousseau writes,

> …I decided to devote my walk of the following day to a self-examination on the subject of falsehood, and I embarked on it in the firm conviction that the 'Know Thyself' of the temple at Delphi was not such an easy precept to observe as I had thought in my *Confessions*. ("Fourth Walk")

To recall this phase of the past, Rousseau is beset by the memory of "a terrible lie" ("Fourth Walk"). Rousseau discovers at this stage that the lie turned out to be more evil in the after-effects – he did not

---

16. The uncanny, according to Freud, "…is related to what is frightening – to what arouses dread and horror…it tends to coincide with what excites fear in general."

    See. *Standard Edition of the Complete Psychological Works of Sigmund Freud: An Infantile Neurosis and Other Works*. Volume XVII, Translated by James Strachey et. al, London: Hogarth Press, 1917-1919. https://uncanny.la.utexas.edu/wp-content/uploads/2016/04/freud-uncanny_001. pdf

know this at the time the lie was told. Rousseau believes that his "innate timidity" ("Fourth Walk") has been the biggest obstacle in his efforts to adhere to his motto of truthfulness in his life, and that the weakness of his nature dictates all other urges of his soul in crucial moments. Rousseau feels that the memory of the lie, which he terms as a "deplorable act," and the "undying remorse" ("Fourth Walk") it has given him, has prevented him from uttering any more falsehoods. Rousseau is surprised to recollect many instances when he had lied without "slightest twinge of regret" ("Fourth Walk"). Rousseau regards it to be a strange contradiction: years of torment for a particular instance of "a careless lie," while several other lies remain in his mind without arousing any compunction. After discovering this problem, he notes that his conscience has always been a faithful guide to him. He cannot understand why one instance of a lie gave him so much guilt and while other instances just went down the memory harmlessly until they were rediscovered by him during self-introspection while walking. Rousseau decides to re-examine his memory to solve this puzzle. He asks: "When and how should one tell the truth to others, since one is not always obliged to tell it? Secondly, are there cases when one can deceive people blamelessly?" ("Fourth Walk")

Though Rousseau regards truth as "the eye of reason" (Fourth Walk"), yet he believes one does not owe the truth to everyone. For Rousseau, "to lie is to conceal a truth which one ought to make known" ("Fourth Walk"). He could excuse someone for concealing the truth in certain circumstances. He decides to examine when and how truth ought to be told to others and situations when one could lie harmlessly. It can be argued that Rousseau's self-examination is similar to the "talking cure" in the psychoanalytical theory, especially the "dream work." In "Dream Work" during the process of "condensation," the "latent elements which have something in common ...[are] combined and fused into a single unity in the manifest dream" ("Dream Work," Freud 278). For instance, in *Reveries*, the image of "the innocent girl" seems to have similarities with Madame de Warens whose memory has been a source of deep psychological trauma for Rousseau ("Tenth Walk"). Therefore, the image of "the innocent girl" by the process of association evokes the painful reactions from the depths of Rousseau's conscience because he has been unconsciously re-enacting the traumatic experience for a long time. Traumatised subjects, observes Linda Belau (qtd. in

Summers-Bremner 309), tend to repeat the traumatic experience unconsciously, without developing an ability to express and assimilate them for a long time. Thus, the incident of a careless lie that caused grief to the girl triggered a re-enactment of the trauma already there in Rousseau's mind.

Returning to the motto of the "Fourth Walk," Rousseau tests the abstract philosophical notion of truth on the touchstone of his felt experience. He begins his meditation with the inquiry about the difference between truth and falsehood, which falsehood is permissible under what circumstances and how much of truth we owe to one another as per the demands of justice and usefulness. Rousseau found vast differences in the theory and practice of truth in contemporary life. He observes that both writers and thinkers tend to utter propound truth in books as it does not involve any risk but, in practice, they are quick to manipulate it to their favour. That is the reason readers find morals in books as "idle impracticable chatter" ("Fourth Walk").

> In its general and abstract sense truth is the most precious of our possessions… But in the particular or individual sense truth is not always such a good thing; sometimes it is a bad thing, and very often it is a matter of indifference. ("Fourth Walk")

First, he considers that we cannot owe somebody a piece of information if it is valueless and therefore useless. Thus, "anyone who conceals or disguises it is not telling a lie" ("Fourth Walk"). Second, for a piece of information to be a lie, it must give rise to injustice. If telling the truth amounts to nothing, the opposite, i.e. telling a lie, will also be of no consequence, therefore, harmless. The basic premise, thus, is that we are "obliged to tell [truth] to others in all matters useful" ("Fourth Walk"): the general truths that a human being needs to carry out his daily life, the truths that advise him/her on the conduct in society, and the truths that guide him/her what they should do and should not do etc. Useless and harmful truths are not supposed to be told to anyone, and hiding such truths does not amount to a lie, any more than relating useful falsehoods. Telling instructional falsehoods is the business of a writers of fables.

Since usefulness differs from person to person, it is necessary to "distinguish between cases where the truth is absolutely required of us, and, those where it can be left unspoken without injustice, and concealed without falsehood" ("Fourth Walk"). Hence, it will certainly not be right to assert that one should always be truthful, regardless of the consequences. Consequences do matter. However, judging a preposition only by the consequences is equally ill-advised. Further, he says that the intention behind the spoken words, not their effects on the listener, is important. For a lie to be innocent, one has to be sure that it will hurt no one. Though it is quite difficult to be sure that it will not do so. Hence, innocent lies are rare and it is difficult to establish that they are so. Therefore, "[t]o lie without advantage or disadvantage to oneself or others is not to lie; it is not falsehood but fiction" ("Fourth Walk").

Rousseau considers the premise that there are allowable and perhaps even desirable falsehoods, which are beneficial for the listener. This is also endorsed by a definition of lying that he has probably read in a philosophical treatise, "to lie is to conceal a truth which one ought to make known" (qtd. by Rousseau, "Fourth Walk"). Accordingly, truth told to a particular person under particular circumstances is a matter of distributive justice. Broadly speaking, remarks Rousseau, "we owe to [sic] each his due" (Gourevitch 497). Rousseau further observes that "[i]n all ethical questions as difficult as this I have always found it best to be guided by the voice of conscience rather than the light of reason. My moral instinct has never deceived me" ("Fourth Walk"). However, conscience has to be nurtured so that it can generate the right signals. Rousseau says he has maintained its purity. If at all he was swayed away from it in a moment of passion, he had been able to regain its authority during self-introspection. Rousseau further adds that he has been judging himself as harshly as he would be judged by God after death.

Innocent falsehoods – innocent as they do not intend injustice to anyone – are falsehoods even though they are harmless. Yet, the voice of his conscience regards justice as equally important to others and the self. Therefore, he feels that by speaking innocent falsehoods, he has hurt his conscience. From clear conscience emerges strong self-respect. Indulging in innocent falsehood amounts to "acquir[ing] the respect of others at the expense of his own" ("Fourth Walk"). Morally instructive fables, which re-organise incidents as a plot to make them more appealing to the readers, should not be called lies. Therefore, a teller of fables as fables is not a liar. However, fables with no moral element told only to entertain and please the reader are lies.

> To lie to one's own advantage is an imposture, to lie to the advantage of others is a fraud, and to lie to the detriment of others is a slander – this is

the worst kind of lie. To lie without advantage or disadvantage to oneself or others is not to lie; it is not falsehood but fiction. ("Fourth Walk")

Rousseau distinguishes "truthfulness" from "prudence" as follows. Prudence keeps personal interest above truth. One can afford to be truthful where personal interest is not involved. However, in personal matters, says Rousseau, people call forth all the gifts of eloquence to make matters look favourable to them. According to Rousseau's doctrine, such types of people are not truthful at all. A truthful person, on the contrary, will never say anything which might favour or disfavour a person against the order of justice and truthfulness – let aside telling a lie. Further, he is "truthful in that he seeks to deceive no one, tell the truth that injures him as faithfully as that which does him credit…" ("Fourth Walk"). Love of truth, says Rousseau, emanates out of love of justice. Both are synonymous for a truthful person. Such a person's heart becomes a shrine where "holy truth," purged of all necessary trivial facts, is forever worshipped. That his superior conscience and self-respect always guide his conduct to be ethical. Rousseau notes that his heart has been following these doctrines intuitively long before he weighed and considered them, and then adopted them as his doctrine. He accepts that he might have lied out of timidity, shame and embarrassment that too in trivial matters, but he has never uttered a "premeditated lie" ("Fourth Walk") to this own advantage or to someone's disadvantage. Finally, Rousseau draws a bottom line that should never be crossed as under:

To give an advantage to someone who does not deserve it is to pervert the order of justice; falsely to attribute to oneself or to another an act which can be praised or blamed, declared innocent or guilty, is to act unjustly; and everything which by being opposed to the truth offends justice in any way is a lie. ("Fourth Walk")

Rousseau says that truth lies at the heart of fiction. When he writes fiction, he keeps moral truths over and above the factual framework of the story. Rousseau considers *Confessions*, an autobiographical work by him, on the touchstone of truth. He says that he had formulated his motto of truth when he wrote *Confessions*. However, even before this when he was writing *Confessions*, he was adhering to these ideals unconsciously. Let alone being careless with respect to details in his autobiography, he judged himself too harshly in matters of adherence to truth. Rousseau, thus, felt assured that when he would have to face God, He would judge him accordingly.

However, he admits lapses in memory in fetching some factual details from the past.

Moreover, some incidents have been deliberately left out, as they would have cast an impression that Rousseau is indulging in self-praise. Finally, Rousseau observes he has always sought guidance from "the moral dictates of [his] conscience than by the abstract notions of truth and falsehood" ("Fourth Walk"). To dedicate one's life to truth prohibits all concessions to inclination, timidity, weakness, shame, or embarrassment. Rousseau sacrificed his comfort and security to his dedication to truth whenever the occasion required, and his present wretched condition results from his truthful conduct. He now feels that he should have sacrificed his weakness and his timidity to it also, and, that insofar as he did not do so his love for truth was a deception. In adopting this motto, he had denied himself the right to certain idle falsehoods. In practice, he fell short of his professed principles. Just as he had lied about and to others out of shame, he had lied about and to himself out of *amour-propre*, i.e. self-respect. That he had been deceiving himself despite his best efforts to be truthful confirms that the Delphic oracle's injunction "know thyself" is not as easy to practise as he had thought when he wrote his *Confessions*. Rousseau's honest admission also justifies Solon's dictum that "it is never too late to learn, even from our enemies, to be wise, truthful, modest and less presumptuous" ("Fourth Walk").

The subject of Rousseau's "Fifth Walk" is happiness. He regards happiness not as a momentary bliss – as ordinary human beings know of it – but as "a single lasting state" ("Fifth Walk"). He states, "our earthly joys are almost without exception the creatures of a moment" ("Fifth Walk") because they are attached to things and times that are liable to change. How can we call such transitory moment happiness? Asks Rousseau. He puts his experience of true happiness thus:

> ...if there is a state where the soul can find a resting-place secure enough to establish itself and concentrate its entire being there, with no need to remember the past or reach into the future, where time is nothing to it, where the present runs on indefinitely but this duration goes unnoticed, with no sign of the passing of time, and no other feeling of deprivation or enjoyment, pleasure or pain, desire or fear than the simple feeling of existence, a feeling that fills our soul entirely, as long as this state lasts, we can call ourselves happy, not with a poor, incomplete and relative happiness such as we find in the pleasures of life, but with a sufficient,

complete and perfect happiness which leaves no emptiness to be filled in the soul. ("Fifth Walk")

The source of such a state of mind, according to Rousseau, has "[n]othing external to us, nothing apart from ourselves and our existence; as long as this state lasts we are self-sufficient like God" ("Fifth Walk"), and ordinary human beings cannot experience such a state because their minds are never calm and free from passion. Thus, Rousseau's experience of happiness is akin to a deep self-meditative state when one is separated from the world of senses.

Williams observes that Rousseau substitutes "a symbolic order for a real one" (qtd. by Burt 231) in his autobiographical works. Rousseau moves to The Saint-Pierre in Switzerland to live in solitude. It is a real as well as spiritual retreat for a philosopher to walk and think in solitude. He studies natural phenomena and finds that every object has spiritual wisdom of its own from which we have shaped our "permanence." To forge a new reality, a philosopher wishes to escape from "permanence" into the fluid and formless nothingness. Thus, Rousseau's visit to the island is a trope on a philosopher's paradise where he can have a "rebirth," and play in the lap of primordial nature. Rousseau's attraction towards water can also be read symbolically. The water conveys the transience of happiness and the continuous flux in human life. During his walks along the bank of the island, Rousseau registers that his mind is flowing like water and is being purged off residual impurities that cause ripples. Rousseau desires to prolong his stay on the island so that he can stay away from the existential predicaments that trouble his mind while living on the mainland ("Fifth Walk").

The "Sixth Walk" begins with an observation that we can unravel the latent motives in our mind that dictate our actions. Rousseau wonders why he has an aversion to a particular path to avoid, which he always takes the roundabout way to reach his destination. When Rousseau searched his mind for discovering the underlying motives behind this reaction, he found the memory of a pauper boy who would approach him for alms, and whom Rousseau would oblige with some money. Slowly, there developed a relationship of "benefactor" and "beneficiary" between them. Whenever Rousseau would pass that way, the boy would approach him, utter praises, and Rousseau would respond with a gift. Initially, Rousseau enjoyed interacting with him. Rousseau's behaviour towards the pauper boy changed into a habit and then into a duty that Rousseau soon started finding irksome. The modus operandi of the pauper boy was like the people who would praise Rousseau to elicit a favour. After the favour, they would, like the pauper boy, enslave their benefactor in a trap of flattery to repeat the favour when they want. This was the reason a pauper boy became so important to impel Rousseau to take the roundabout way instead.

This discovery underlines the psychoanalytical concept that the human mind "condenses" two similar images into one. ("Dream Work," Fraud 279). In this example, Rousseau wants to avoid the pauper boy in the same way he used to evade the tricksters who wanted to dupe him. When Rousseau thinks of the pauper boy who behaves like a trickster, his mind reacts likewise to stay away from him. This reaction has similarities with Rousseau's overwhelming feeling of guilt for "the innocent girl" and another image of "the little girl" ("Ninth Walk") selling apples to oblige whom he buys all her apples. After making this discovery, Rousseau deliberates on the notion of charity as an abstract ethical concept vis-à-vis his personal experience of practising charity.

Rousseau takes the abstract idea of charity to test it on his felt experience. Rousseau admits he enjoys doing charity the most when his heart longs for it. But his experience teaches him that good deeds may have an evil consequence. Earlier, Rousseau enjoyed doing charity following the "impulses of [his] heart," yet after every charitable act, he felt burdened with a responsibility to repeat the favour in future when the beneficiary wants it. This way, says Rousseau, his "dearest pleasures" became "burdensome responsibilities" ("Sixth Walk"). As a result, he earned the reputation of a universal benefactor of all the needy people (or who thought they were "needy" and only Rousseau's help could rescue them from their problem). Then he finds that even tricksters in search of a dupe approached him. Thus, his good deeds served the interests of bad people. The realisation dawns on him that acts of charity practised blindly do not amount to good. Therefore, the light of reason should guide our acts of charity.

A good deed is never good when it results in serving the wicked designs of an evil person. Thus, Rousseau concludes, "all our natural impulses, including even charity itself, can change their nature when we import them into society and follow them unthinkingly...the only good which is henceforth within [his] power is to abstain from acting lest unwittingly and unintentionally I should act badly" ("Sixth

Walk"). Goodness done as a part of the duty or done under compulsion rarely delights him. In the past, he thought that charity for inner pleasure results from his virtuous nature. But there is no virtue in "doing good just when you feel like it" ("Sixth Walk") because virtue consists in subduing your pleasure for the sake of duty, not vice versa.

Sometimes Rousseau has a mind to punish the thankless people who reward his charity with hate, but he cannot do so because he is powerless. Even if he had the power to punish the guilty, he would not have done it because he cannot convince himself to act to anyone's harm. Therefore, he abstains from all action. For Rousseau, becoming powerful means becoming more tolerant, free from hate and the desire for revenge. Rousseau confesses that seeking pleasure is his nature, and he cannot do anything that does not afford pleasure. Rousseau says that a "purely voluntary deed" is something that he enjoys doing the best. And when anyone does a favour to another, both the benefactor and the beneficiary enter into an unwritten contract that the benefactor would continue the same favour if the recipient remains worthy of it, and the benefactor can afford to repeat the same favour later also.

> [W]hen the recipient uses it as a claim on further favours and rewards me with hate if I refuse, when he insists on my being his perpetual benefactor just because I initially took pleasure in helping him, then charity becomes burdensome and pleasure vanishes. ("Sixth Walk")

How can Rousseau be nice to people when their behaviour is wicked? To be nice to people as a matter of formality is not in Rousseau's nature. Perhaps he has changed a lot as he matured. His experiences of twenty years prove that good deeds may attract harmful consequences, and this bitter experience has so degraded his soul that he fears every good deed might lead to evil results either by chance or by the designs of cunning people. Maybe Rousseau's adverse experiences have hardened him. There are, according to Rousseau, two types of adversities: one that ennobles and enlightens and the other that crushes the soul and depraves it. But the hardships he has faced were the hardest and soul-crushing ones. Rousseau remembers when he received the first shock, which shattered his innocence and made him rethink practising charity. From then onwards, notes Rousseau, he has become so suspicious of not only his own natural inclinations but of clever men who are eager to manipulate them to their advantage. Despite this, he has not grown hateful of those people because he does not want to corrupt his soul; he only wants to avoid them. Rousseau muses if he could live among his detractors invisibly or unrecognisably, he could still "display a universal and disinterested benevolence" ("Sixth Walk") towards them because weakness and vulnerability give rise to hatred and vengefulness. If he had been strong and all-powerful like God, he would have been benevolent and forgiving like Him. "Strength and freedom," notes Rousseau, nurture goodness in humans, whereas "weakness and slavery" create evildoers ("Sixth Walk").

Rousseau reflects that, because of his independent nature, he has always been a misfit in society. He cannot do charity as a matter of duty because that does not afford the pleasure of a selfless voluntary act. When he is under external pressure to do something he does not like, he abstains from doing it at all. Human freedom, states Rousseau, does not comprise doing what one wants, rather "never doing what one *does not* (emphasis added) want to do" ("Sixth Walk"). Human beings living under the yoke of societal conformity hardly have any freedom to do what they want. Harder still is to know what they want to do because that prerequisites self-knowledge. Rousseau believes that we can solve this puzzle by approaching it negatively, i.e. by avoiding doing what we do not want to do – though that is not so easy either.

Rousseau comes to the awareness that this freedom has been his real nemesis all his life. He has been surrounded by people who spend their lives doing what they do not wish to do. They do it to get power over other people whom they, in turn, force to do something against their will. In this way, says Rousseau, people end up doing acts against their better selves just for grabbing power to have command over others. Anyone who refuses to participate in this game is made an object of derision and hate. Though he has never done premeditated evil in his life, people regard his very presence as detrimental to society. His sins are the sins of omission, not the sins of commission. He concludes the "Sixth Walk" proudly, claiming that perhaps he has done less evil than any person living in his times has.

In the "Seventh Walk," Rousseau rediscovers his former passion for taking "botanical walks." He states that taking pleasure in a hobby is a sign of a peaceful mind, and that by being happy, he can score a victory over his detractors who want to see him in pain ("Seventh Walk"). Rousseau decides to find out the reason behind the renewal of his interest in botany in the last stage of his life in terms of whether it has anything to do with self-knowledge. Rousseau recalls the times when he would take pleasure in reveries and be uninterested in worldly fame and fortune. Rousseau's reverie is more akin to meditation than thinking.

> [R]everie amuses and distracts me, thought wearies and depresses me; thinking has always been for me a disagreeable and thankless occupation. Sometimes my reveries end in meditation, but more often my meditations end in reverie, and during these wanderings my soul roams and soars through the universe on the wings of imagination, in ecstasies which surpass all other pleasures. ("Seventh Walk")

Rousseau fears that the traumas he had suffered at the hands of his tormentors would dull his imaginative faculties, and that he may not be able to enjoy reveries like before, but walking helps him heal his mind and recover the lost pleasure in reveries once again. He shares his experience thus:

> In these circumstances an instinct that is natural to me averted my eyes from every depressing thought, silenced my imagination and, fixing my attention on the objects surrounding me, made me look closely for the first time at the details of the great pageant of nature, which until then I had hardly ever contemplated otherwise than as a total and undivided spectacle. ("Seventh Walk")

In the earlier walks, Rousseau hardly noticed the natural flora and fauna, as he was too preoccupied with traumatic memories of his past. The external collage of natural objects described in "Seventh Walk" can be regarded as a sign of inner healing. In this walk, he not only begins to register the sensuous stimuli of nature around him but, also, despite his frail physique, wishes to botanise like he used to when he was young, and when his mind was free from sorrows, is a testimony that he has "walked away" from his painful past. After a long time, he is feeling light-hearted and ready to enjoy his life again. To quote Paul de Man, "The sensory manifestation of art and literature is the outside of an inner content which is itself an outer event or entity that has been internalised" (771). Rousseau regards worldly name and fame as burdensome and wants to live a life dedicated to the pleasures of the soul. To quote Marcel Raymond,

> [T]here are crucial places in the *Reveries* where the natural ground is cut away to reveal a vast subterranean network, an underground city. Such passages...show the self's encounter with itself in nature to be a pretext for the uncovering of an allegory of a reader confronting a structure like a text. [In]... the Seventh Promenade where Rousseau explains why he loves to botanise and recounts a series of examples, apparently to demonstrate the premise that it is in front of the *book of nature* (emphasis

> added) rather than writing his *Reveries* that he is happiest. (Raymond qtd. in Burt 232)

Rousseau notes he could not connect with nature when his heart was "constricted by misery and gathered all its impulses tightly around itself" ("Seventh Walk"). The moment he stops identifying with his traumatic memories and starts establishing a bond with the natural surroundings, the process of his healing quickens. Harmony and order in nature have a divine unity that a person who is "ready" for it can register. The "readiness" comes from rising above the egoistic perception.

Rousseau identifies anthropocentrism as one reason behind humankind's inability to connect with nature spiritually. People are interested in nature insofar as it can serve their material interests and help them cure their illnesses. Influenced by the human-centred view of nature (which is rooted in Cartesian philosophy), we regard nature as nothing more than a physical resource to be exploited by human beings. Rousseau calls for "disinterested contemplation" ("Seventh Walk") of nature because approaching nature for satisfying one's needs prevents a purely spiritual experience of it.

Rousseau says that he has always wished for universal happiness for one and all until he discovered that "malicious men" ("Seventh Walk") had their happiness in his sorrow. He would prefer being solitary in the lap of nature, the "eternal mother" than in the company of treacherous people. Rousseau wants to live an authentic life as a solitary walker in nature. People have to repress their true nature to play roles imposed upon them by society. Rousseau calls it "death in life." He wants his soul to flower in the company of nature and experience the ecstatic enjoyment of communion with "the eternal spirit." Rousseau's "nature" is not purely external rather, it is external and internal in perfect harmony ("Seventh Walk").

> Botany is the ideal study for the idle, unoccupied solitary; a blade and a magnifying glass are all the equipment he needs for his observations. He wanders about, passing freely from one object to another, he considers each plant in turn with interest and curiosity, and as soon as he begins to grasp the laws of their structure he receives from his observations an effortless pleasure as intense as if it had cost him a great deal of labour. This ideal occupation has a charm which can only be felt when the passions are entirely at rest ("Seventh Walk").

The experience of knowing nature through intuition is best exemplified in several fine passages from the *Reveries* in which Rousseau gives himself over to the rhythms of nature and allows his very being to settle into these motions. Rousseau's *Reveries* rejects the view of nature as an object of study by humans. Nor does Rousseau approve of studying nature to write about it. To come to terms with the memory of "men and the attacks of the wicked," Rousseau dedicates himself to walking and thinking ("Seventh Walk").

> The more sensitive the soul of the observer, the greater the ecstasy aroused in him by this harmony. At such times, his senses are possessed by a deep and delightful reverie, and in a blissful self-abandonment, he loses himself in the immensity of this beautiful order, with which he feels himself at one. All individual objects escape him; he sees and feels nothing but the unity of things. His ideas have to be restricted and his imagination limited by some particular circumstances for him to observe the separate parts of this universe, which he was trying to embrace in its entirety. ("Seventh Walk")

Rousseau's *Reveries* testify that walking is the most natural way to approach nature, and that the natural environment is the place where humans truly belong and that a natural setting is the most appropriate place for spreading out the intimate layers of the self for reconsideration and reconciliation. "I prefer the harshest solitude to the society of malicious men which thrives only on treachery and hate" ("Seventh Walk"). Lane and Clark also observe that …

> Rousseau's works contain a comprehensive reconsideration of the fundamental character of the human animal, the causes of historical changes in human behaviour, and a credible account of the process by which these changes altered humans' relationship to the natural world. Rousseau shows how these changes have been harmful; that is, how man's estrangement from nature is fundamentally linked to his estrangement from his own natural (i.e., physical) self as well as from other (human and nonhuman) beings. (63)

In the "Eight Walk," Rousseau asserts that if he had adopted ways of the world, he would have been outwardly happy, but true happiness would always be beyond his reach. In the "Eight Walk," Rousseau again recalls traumatic experiences of the past and bemoans the sense of dejection and waste associated with it. Rousseau begins the "Eighth Walk" with a paradoxical observation that the spells of happiness in his life failed to give him comforting memories, whereas moments of adversity not only cast a lasting impression on his consciousness but also transformed those experiences into pleasant memories. Despite having all the worldly name and fame, observes Rousseau, he knew he was not happy; he lived relatively peacefully when his senses were turned inwards. On the contrary, even in his present "deplorable circumstances," he would not trade places with the happiest and most prosperous person. He observes that "adversity" compels us to think about our past and us. That is why most people get scared of adversity. Rousseau does not worry because he has never done "premeditated evil" ("Eighth Walk").

Rousseau states he has learned to look at his appalling situation with "near-indifference" ("Eighth Walk"). Even amid misfortunes, Rousseau can possess his peace of mind, which has happened not miraculously but by a natural process of healing. The instinct that rebelled against enduring the adversities patiently was Rousseau's self-love. During his "Eighth Walk," Rousseau discovers that his self-love was not ready for passive suffering because of indignation towards his tormentors. Therefore, it took him some time before he could win over his self-love[17] to achieve true happiness. Humiliations affect those the most who overthink about them. Someone whose self-esteem does not depend on the opinion of others stays peacefully unaffected by all indignities hurled at him by people. Rousseau shares his experience of learning to rein in his senses:

> Only when I had detached myself from the social passions and their dismal train did I find her once again in all her beauty. Convinced of the impossibility of repressing these first involuntary reactions, I have given up the attempt. Whenever I am provoked, I allow my blood to boil and my senses to be possessed by anger and indignation; I give way to this first explosion of nature, which all my efforts could not prevent or impede. I merely try to stop it leading to any undesirable consequences. My eyes flash, my face flares up, my limbs tremble and palpitations choke me; these are all purely physical reactions and reasoning has no effect on them, but once nature has had this initial explosion one can become one's own master again and gradually regain control over one's senses; this is what I have tried to do, for a long time to no avail, but eventually with greater success. ("Eight Walk")

This patient indifference to everything, including life and death, says Rousseau, is the reward that he has received for his long-suffering. This blissful nonchalance gives him the impression of living in "prosperity" amid "adversity." According to Rousseau, malicious people affect him negatively; living away from such people

---

17 Self-love sometimes manifests itself as self-esteem or love of self or even petty pride. Love of self as against self-love is a positive state of mind. It happens when one is aware of one's surroundings as well as one's self as mutually connected entities. This state is achieved when the instinct of self-love is conquered.

is the only way to be happy. Rousseau shares his experience of happy moments during solitary walks in the country, "…as soon as I am under the trees and surrounded by greenery, I feel as if I were in the earthly paradise and experience an inward pleasure as intense as if I were the happiest of men ("Eight Walk"). The "Eighth Walk" reiterates the earlier confession that his tormentors cannot affect him but temporarily. They cannot shock him out of his senses, but for a while, and they can never touch his soul. Though Rousseau recovers his peace of mind again, the fear that the disquietude may revisit him remains.

In the "Ninth Walk," Rousseau returns to the idea of happiness. He notes that happiness is not for the inhabitants of this world – not at least in the way they think of it. Human beings cannot be permanently happy because they attach their happiness to situations that change; only the self-contented people have a feeling akin to happiness, and they are rare. Rousseau recollects memories of happy moments from the past, showing that happiness is a subjective, rare, but contagious emotion. Then he recounts an incident when he had to listen to an obituary in which the reader gratuitously mentioned that lack of love and affection for one's children is a sign of depravity and cruel heart, and that a person who hates children is a potential criminal. Rousseau feels that the reader of the obituary had said it on purpose. He wanted to taunt Rousseau for not loving his children as Rousseau had put his children away in Foundlings' Home. This incident evokes a long monologue from Rousseau on his decision not to keep his children with him. Rousseau feels people might be misrepresenting him as an "unnatural father" ("Ninth Walk") who has put his children in a childcare home. He wonders at human ingenuity to malign people's reputations by sheer misrepresentation. Then, he recalls the happy times when he was with his children. He also justifies his decision to put his children in a childcare home – not with himself, not with his wife and her family – because as a father he knew where his children would get the best education.

Rousseau says that he likes children so much that all his knowledge of the human heart could be attributed to his love of children. However, later on, his growing age and failing faculties came in the way of his spending more time with children. Since children also dislike extremely old and haggard faces, Rousseau does not force them to give him company if they do not like it. Yet, he still longs for seeing that rapturous expression of happiness in a child's eyes and would even like to hold a little child in his arms if he gets an opportunity. Happiness muses Rousseau, sometimes exudes a person's overall being, sometimes it laughs through somebody's laugh, and at times, it is projected into the heart through somebody's glance. Happiness is a contagious emotion, and it spreads from one heart to another quickly. He states that while contentment is easier to recognise, happiness is more elusive and elf-like.

Happiness for Rousseau begins with making others happy, and from their happiness, one can derive one's happiness. He recounted an incident when he had bought all the apples from a young girl to offer a chance to the entire company to enjoy themselves. Happiness is first projected to then it reflects on the giver. Moreover, happiness, according to Rousseau, is of a moral origin. Happiness derived from inflicting pain on somebody is not true happiness because happiness cannot have pain at its basis. To quote, "signs of pleasure on the faces of evildoers are nothing but signs that their malice is satisfied. Innocent joy is the only joy whose appearance delights my heart" ("Ninth Walk"). Happiness and sadness affect him more because Rousseau's being extends to embrace the sufferer. Sometimes he suffers worse than the person who is actually in pain. Rousseau states that when he is all alone, he is completely himself; he is strongly affected when he is near people who are in pain. That is why he wants to keep aloof from other people. But he has become so infamous because of a "universal" hate campaign against him it has become impossible to roam around incognito. Wherever he goes, people sneer at him as if he were their worst enemy. Nevertheless, even amid bad people, he finds some kind souls, which give him hope.

It is erroneous to say that "Tenth Walk" is fragmentary. No other walk is as whole and real as the "Tenth Walk" because Rousseau reaches inner peace and serenity in the "Tenth Walk."

> There is not a day when I do not remember with joy and loving emotion that one short time in my life when I was myself, completely myself, unmixed and unimpeded, and when I can genuinely claim to have lived. ("Tenth Walk")

The "Tenth Walk" is "real" because everything, "unreal," has been peeled away during the previous walks. Therefore, the experience contained in the "Tenth Walk" can be regarded as the "kernel" of his self (Lacan 53). The "Tenth Walk" recollects the time Rousseau had spent with Madame de Warens. This walk stands in sharp contrast to earlier walks in tone and tenor. The belligerent and tormented soul of Rousseau has now become serene and calm. The tender way the memories of the time spent with Madame de Warens are related in this walk shows that they have been very delicately preserved of all Rousseau's treasure of memorable experiences. This experience would decide what kind of human being he would become. To quote him, "... [T]his first impulse determined my whole life and led inexorably to the fate that has governed the rest of my days" (Rousseau).

As posited by Sigmund Freud and Jacques Lacan, the concept of trauma is essential to understand Rousseau's *Reveries*. "We describe as 'traumatic' any external excitations that are powerful enough to break through the protective shield. It seems...that the concept of trauma necessarily implies a connection with a breach in an otherwise efficacious barrier against stimuli. Such events, as external trauma, are bound to provoke a disturbance on a large scale in the functioning of the organism's energy and to set in motion every possible defensive measure" (*Pleasure Principle*, Freud 23). Thus, by being beyond the symbolic, trauma keeps on destabilising the symbolic order in a big way. So long as the subject cannot express the trauma (in the language of the symbolic), it continues to have hysterical symptoms whose intensity varies from case to case and person-to-person ("*Beginning the Treatment*," Freud 27).

It can thus be argued that we should not take at face value the fact that everyone was unjust to Rousseau. Because when Rousseau thought they victimised him under "a universal conspiracy," he was, in fact, "loved, admired and revered by many of his contemporaries" (France). It can be argued that Rousseau's wholesale condemnation of all as his tormentors is the work of his "frenzied imagination" (France) because of some underlying trauma. The time he had spent with Madame de Warens forms the basis of the trauma he has to excavate and confront. With an encounter with Madame Warens, he was prematurely shaken out of "innocence" into "experience," which at that tender age his body did not have the "apparatus" to handle, nor did it ever develop the capability to cope with it later on; it affected his soul deeply without ever being properly assimilated. This sedimentation of the irreconcilable trauma brought forth consequences he suffered throughout his life. But walking and thinking provided Rousseau with a way to gain access to the depths of his troubled self and helped him heal it slowly. This exercise of self-psychoanalysis, with walking in the background, not only helped him heal himself of the trauma by accessing, assimilating and finally narrating it, but also provided him with the knowledge of how his deep mind worked.

It is easy to notice that all the walks by Rousseau follow the cyclical and repetitive narrative structure: he begins with a re-look at his past, relives the trauma he has endured, feels dejected, endeavours to rationalise the traumatic experience, recovers from it and becomes himself again. Even the past, present and future are so mixed up that they seem to merge in the eternal continuum. Since Rousseau is both the patient and the analyst, every walk can be split into two parts: one comprising confession/expression of traumatic experiences – that he repeats almost in every walk – by Rousseau, the patient; and the other comprising rationalisation/reconciliation of the trauma by Rousseau, the analyst. Each walk concludes with a sense of satisfaction of having overcome at least some of the troubling memories of the past. Thus, Rousseau, by practising walking and thinking, gets over the burden of his traumatic past and regains peace of mind before his death.

CHAPTER 2

Walking and the Art of Living: Henry David Thoreau's *Walden* and "Walking"

The experience of human beings as dwellers in nature has been largely forgotten. Since the beginning of a settled way of life, complains Thoreau, the civilised human being has overshadowed his/her precursor, the "sojourner in nature" ("Walking") in art and literature. Thoreau recommends walking in the wild to excavate and relive that experience stored in the collective human memory. With walking, suggests Thoreau, the walker can time-travel in the mind to the phase just before the arrival of the civilised way of life in the human evolutionary journey. In the essay "Walking," Thoreau demonstrates that walking in nature can help us reconnect with the pre-civilised way of life once again. How can walking do it? One might ask. Walking, which Thoreau speaks of, has nothing to do with physical exercise. The practice of walking as art, argues Thoreau, helps in exploring the deep mind to unravel that buried experience in the collective unconscious[18] of the human race, which is free from any cultural conditioning. All subsequent utterances about walking in the essay can be understood in this perspective. However, walking is not so much a physical act of putting one step in front of another, as it is a mixed metaphor of movement in diverse directions in the non-

18 A walker has to relive the experiences of human beings as "sojourner[s] in nature" in the collective unconscious. Propounded by C. G. Jung, the term, the collective unconscious, is that part of the conscious, which contains archetypes or universal images that are shared by all humankind. It is different from personal unconscious, in the sense that personal unconscious contains the memories of individual experiences.

See. Collective Unconscious, *Encyclopaedia Britannica*, Encyclopaedia Britannica Press, 2020, https://www.britannica.com/science/collective-unconscious, July 09, 2020.

physical sense as well. Nevertheless, there is a subtle play between the physical and the transcendental aspects of walking and therein lies the "absolute freedom and wildness" ("Walking") of a walker. In other words, the act of walking is to reconnect dispersed fragments of experience encountered along the way for the purpose of reconstituting a whole. To turn the metaphor further, walking is like an *invisible* thread joining the scattered beads of a broken rosary together.

Thoreau observes that any walking saint, who undertakes to walk to the "Holy Land" (a geographical destination) is jestingly regarded either as the "Sainte-Terrer," a "Holy Lander," or as a "sans terre," someone who does not have a "home" a particular place and is always on the move. However, adds Thoreau, he is a walker in "good sense." Thoreau finds a saint's walking similar to his own practice of walking because a walking saint leaves "home" behind forever before s/he sets out. Thoreau views "Holy Land," the idealised land, as a metaphor for a particular state of consciousness, since such travelling would divest the walker not only of "home" as a particular place but also all the cultural, social, national identities that "home" invokes. Walking to the "Holy Land" is to abandon a settled mode of life. According to Thoreau, a walker has to rediscover in himself/herself the original "sojourner in nature" in order to relive the experience of the human ancestors before they embraced such a mode of life. Thoreau cautions that once a walker gains access to the deep mind, there is no stopping and no return because walking takes control of the walker. In other words, a walker "arrives" if he is able to reverse the binary between walker and walking, and once walking takes over the walker, there is no return: "If you are ready to leave father and mother, and brother and sister, and wife and child and friends, and never see them again – if you have paid your debts, and made your will, and settled all your affairs, and are a free man, then you are ready for a walk" ("Walking"). This implies some puzzling questions: Is walking such a risky proposition that one has to write his will before setting out? What does Thoreau mean by "readiness" to walk? Whether or not these words echo Shakespeare's "ripeness is all" (*King Lear*, Act V, Sc II, p. 174, line 11), the question stands. If it means maturity in years, why does Thoreau start walking – begin a quest for the lost knowledge – at a young age of 34 or so?[19] The answer seems to lie in another question. At what point in time should one ideally start walking? Since Thoreau was deeply influenced by the classical Sanskrit literature, especially the epics, the concept of *varnasramadharama*[20] (Basu 30), which is central to the Hindu religio-philosophical writings, would be relevant to explain the point. *Vanaprastha* is the last of the four stages in the orderly unfolding of human life as envisaged in the Vedic *varnasramadharama* system. If so, then why does Thoreau want to disrupt the established order by setting out on a walk at a young age? If *vanaprasthana* is meant for a retired person who has fulfilled all his duties in the earlier three phases of life, why does Thoreau decide to walk the path ordained for a retiree? These are some of the questions this chapter will explore with reference to "Walking" and *Walden.* It is remarkable that "Walking" reveals the background of *Walden*; some of the motifs, especially the leitmotif of the practice of walking, which were behind the scene in *Walden* (1854), are brought out in "Walking" (1861). In other words, the dynamics of the art of walking and thinking are put forth in "Walking;" whereas in *Walden*, it is the product, not the practice of walking and thinking, which is foregrounded.

Let us take up the first question. What does Thoreau mean by walking? As mentioned above, walking and solitary living are the two enabling practices in Thoreau's spiritual and philosophical journey in the woods. Though he sometimes compromises with the latter as he receives quite a few visitors at his Cabin in Walden, he practises walking every day religiously; hence, it merits particular attention. Elsewhere, he says, "the swiftest traveller is he that goes afoot" (*Walden* 53). Obviously, he is not talking about walking as a physical act of moving from place A to place B only. Rather he is considering walking as a consciously evolutionary human act, as an act that

19 If we presume that he started walking, when he wrote *Walden,* i.e. he was not walking earlier than he began his experiment at the Walden Pond, then, we can say, he began practising walking at the age of 34.

20 *Varnasramadharama* is a Hindu Vedic prescription on the conduct of human life, defining the orderly unfolding of human life in four stages: *brahmacari-ashram,* studentship; *Grihasta,* the family life after marriage; *Vanaprashta;* life as a hermit in retreat, and *Sannyasa*, life as a wandering ascetic. Jogiraj Basu quoted by Patrick Olivelle.

See. Olivelle, Patrick. *The Asrama System: The History and Hermeneutics of a Religious Institution.* Oxford University Press, 1993. Print.

influenced our evolution deeply as when our ancestors walked their way from their fellow species to become the masters of the planet. For this reason, a brief look at the evolutionary history of walking is necessary.

Unwritten anywhere in history books, the hi(story) of walking writes itself in human anatomy (Amato 21). Walking on two feet might have necessitated erect posture, which reshaped the human pelvis and limbs. The anatomy shaped by bipedalism not only set hominids apart from other species in terms of posture but also allowed them "to make a fuller use of their breath and vocal chords, enabling them to issue more complex and diverse sounds than their sniffing and panting cousins…" (21). The ability to walk seems to have helped develop the competence for speech. The rhythms of walking probably led to the making of accompanying sounds, which eventually assumed the form of language and song. Amato cites Robert Provine who claims that "hominids had to walk before they could talk" (21). He further observes, significantly, that perhaps this song and rhyme evolved not only to sustain them on their long walks across landscapes but also allowed them to weave narratives about the places they walked through. Therefore, it can be argued that bipedal locomotion produced the conditions for humans to develop the capacity to walk and talk at the same time and, thus, for the creation of song and story (22).

Moreover, walking as movement on foot is different from travel, as one can travel around the world yet not move at all. What the movement on foot can give, travelling in a vehicle cannot give at all. It is the body propelled-locomotion, and the sights, scents and scenes as well as the people one meets on the way that make the movement experientially special. Rebecca Solnit says that in this way, walking becomes ambivalent and enormously creative, and, in a sense, the walker "arrives" as soon as the first step is taken (ch. 1). Walking through sights and scenes allows the mind to connect the internal and abstract with the external and concrete, to join the familiar with the new, to form new thought-compounds. Hence, walking has been an indispensable activity for thinkers through the ages and the history of walking has been inextricably associated with the history of thinking and writing. Walking physically is to "move at a regular pace by lifting and setting down each foot in turn, never having both feet off the ground at once."[21] However, it is not the physicality of walking only that is our central concern. On the contrary, it is walking, except for its physicality, which is crucial from our point of view. It can be termed as transcendental walking, which Thoreau alludes to when he says that the art of walking comes to a walker "only by the grace of God," that such walkers are "the chosen" ones belonging the "select class" of human beings, and that a walker, in this sense, must be born into the family of "the Walkers" ("Walking"). In this way, walking is neither travel in the physical sense, nor an exercise, nor a pastime. Yet, the physical aspect of walking is an indispensable precondition for transcendental walking to happen. One can understand it with the help of an analogy: physical walking is the root, while transcendental walking is the fruit. To put it differently, the physical act of walking is the science of walking, while transcendental walking is the art of walking. It is the union of physical and transcendental walking, and the union of walker with walking, that produces embodied experience, which is the hallmark of the literature of walking. Such experience is unique to the person yet embedded in the place. In a nutshell, a walker experiences his thoughts sensuously to arrive at what can be termed as experiential thinking. If walking is so easy and universal, why does Thoreau declare it an art that only those blessed by God can practise? Walking, observes Thoreau, is an art lost long ago when human beings ceased to be walkers in nature; this lost art needs to be rediscovered. But only the practice of walking can rediscover the art of walking because in it is hidden the secret of poise between the mind and the body perfected for millions of years since human ancestors first scrambled to their two feet.

Who will discover it? An ordinary walker begins walking on the physical plane and ends it on the physical plane itself. The walking artist, too, no doubt, begins it as a physical act, but he knows how to take off and float in the transcendental realm, and it is in this realm that the walking artist is able to think creatively. Tim Ingold terms it as "the experience of weather" (122), which, he asserts, has a significant bearing on one's state of mind, which in turn stimulates creative thinking. Thoreau states that the transcendental plane is the heavenly plane of walking, to enter which the walker requires "direct dispensation from heaven" ("Walking"). And this is the reason

---

21 See *Oxford Dictionary of English*, Third Edition.

Thoreau never attempts to define walking in positive terms; he only approaches it in negative terms, so that walking is kept out of the trinity of power as the "fourth estate," never to be appropriated by institutions like "church, state and the people" ("Walking"). In other words, he does not want walking to be put under "institutional closure" (Caputo 333) by imposing a definition on it.

The physical and transcendental concept of walking may be further understood in the light of the psychoanalytical view of the mind. According to Freud, a large part of the mind is unconscious, consisting of instinctual wishes and repressed desires that, despite being unconscious, have a strong influence on the conscious mind of an individual.[22] The unconscious always undercuts the conscious mind. This elusive equilibrium between the two provides the primary environment for creative thinking. Annie Dillard confesses the unconscious can neither be silenced nor ignored, only allowed to flow (Dillard).[23] How can walking help achieve and sustain this equilibrium? We have enough archaeological and paleontological evidence to support the hypothesis that walking is not only unique to the human species but also is an unparalleled achievement in terms of the use of the human mind coupled with a perfect alignment with the human body for achieving the gravity-defying, erect movement on two legs. The human mind and body both have to reach a precise balance to achieve the feat of erect walking. It is no less than a revolution in the hi(story) of human evolution. Moreover, findings in the field of clinical research establish that walking movements are achieved when babies are still in the womb at the seventeenth week, when the cortex, the part of the brain responsible for thinking, is not yet functional (Nicholson 11),[24] suggesting that walking is the function of the unconscious mind. The equilibrium between the unconscious and the conscious, which is so essential for thinking, is achieved when the unconscious mind is pleasurably engaged (Pamela 85-86).[25] Moreover, practising walking, as an art, stirs libido

22 Thurschwell, Pamela. *Sigmund Freud, Routledge Critical Thinkers: Essential Guides for Literary Studies*, Routledge, London, 2001, p 4, EBook.

23 See, chapter "Seeing" in Dillard, Annie. *Pilgrim at Tinker Creek*, Harper Collins, United Kingdom, 1974. EBook.

24 Nicholson, Geoff. *The Lost Art of Walking*. p 11. Print.

25 Freud maintains that libido is always inclined towards pleasure. Therefore, if it has to be engaged in walking, it must have an element of pleasure in it.

pleasurably (Forel and Fetscher 209),[26] which can lead to the opening of a brave new world of awareness about oneself vis-à-vis the surroundings. It is this function of walking that Thoreau evokes in his essay "Walking." Why does Thoreau begin walking at a relatively young age? The question relates to *Walden* as much as to "Walking." Thoreau responds to this question in *Walden*. He says he took the radical step when he could not find an established teacher-disciple tradition in his times, which could initiate him in the search for self-knowledge. To put it simply, when Thoreau found no archetypal wise old man (Stein 202-203)[27] having first-hand experience of such spiritual quest, he felt impelled to set forth alone. This disruption of chronology[28] has far-reaching consequences (Parkhill 133), and that is why Thoreau forewarns any dilettante aspiring to follow his path.

Thoreau notes that William Wordsworth, the romantic poet, would first get a feel of his thoughts before writing them down. It was in his walking-and-thinking sessions across the Lake District that he composed most of his poems. Relating thought to experience, Thoreau observes that thought should bear the same relation to

---

See. Thurschwell, Pamela. *Sigmund Freud*, Routledge Critical Thinkers: Essential Guide for Literary Studies, Routledge, London, 2001, EBook, p. 85-86.

26 Walter Benjamin cites his youthful experiences of practising walking in the city of Berlin. He discovers that walking can transform the way the city is experienced by the walker; it can even lend sexual appeal to inanimate objects on the cityscape. During one of those casual walks to explore the city, he "discovers his own libido."

See. McElligott, Anthony. Editor, *The German Urban Experience: Modernity and its Crisis, 1900-1945*, Routledge, 2001, Digital Edition, 2005. p. 209.

27 Thoreau cites "the failure of the old men of his culture to pass on to the succeeding generations an enduring legacy of wisdom." He is longing for the "guru-shishya parampara" (translation mine) of the East in America. Voicing his strong spiritual relation with the East, he wonders elsewhere, "[W]as not Asia mapped in my brain before it was in any geography?"

See. Scott, David. *Rewalking Thoreau and Asia: "Light from the East 'for' A Very Yankee Sort of Oriental."*

28 Thoreau decided to go walking at the age when he ought to be absorbed in his family life. His case has echoes with that of Pāndavas in *The Mahabharata*, who were forced into exile by treachery of their cousins. This disruption in the orderly unfolding of life of the princes eventually has catastrophic consequences for the entire dynasty.

See. Parkhill, Thomas. "Going to the Forest: The Case of the Pāndavas."

experience as the day bears to the night and the summer to the winter. Abstract thought can be compared to "indoor" study while practising walking with a thought in the mind is like testing the thought on the touchstone of felt experience. In other words, Thoreau invites sedentary thinkers/philosophers to take a walk with a thought in the mind in order to experience it sensuously before presenting it to the readers. Staying indoors makes one oversensitive to impressions so that even raw, unfelt thoughts tend to be presented to the reader. A thought is raw when it is not sensuously experienced by the thinker. A thought, to be experiential, must be felt by a walking/wakeful body. And it is this walking/wakeful body that Thoreau takes along on his long walks as a companion.

The walker in the woods has to be mindful of his surroundings with an aim to connect with them sensuously. Walking in the woods, says Thoreau, while "thinking out of woods" is of no use. Sharing his outdoor walking experience, Thoreau notes that walking can cast a veil of creative unfamiliarity over a familiar landscape. As a result, the walker can discover immense creative potentialities in a given radius. Thoreau bemoans the cutting down of forests and the erection of fences resulting in a fragmentation of the landscape. A walker desires an expanse of open land to walk freely. Thoreau states that he can walk any number of miles – ten, fifteen, twenty. The mention of miles walked in the wild, away from human dwelling, seems to be another benchmark for a walker. In other words, Thoreau seems to suggest that after having done twenty miles in the woods the walker starts *thinking* (emphasis mine). The literature of walking captures the actual walking trail of the walker with all the twists and turns in the narrative of the text. For example, in "Walking," Thoreau's walking away from the civilisation into the woods is accompanied by a parallel switch of thoughts, which involves a sharpened awareness to view the human civilisation from the perspective of an outsider. In other words, the walker is able to somewhat distance him/herself from the cultural conditioning to rediscover the traces of pre-cultural human nature. Thoreau decries the change of public lands into private property, which brings restrictions on free walking. His words sound prophetic when one considers what has happened since the global dominance of privatisation of public spaces, "[L]et us improve our opportunities, then, before the evil days come" ("Walking").

The difference between walking indoors and outdoors presupposes a "house." Is it the same house that the walker has left behind before setting out? Thoreau employs the word "house" as a complex metaphor in "Walking" and, also, in *Walden*. Though initially in "Walking" Thoreau regards a "house" as a physical structure and a place of dwelling, he endows it also with the richness of a deep metaphor. One of the most sustained and elaborately developed tropes in *Walden* is the "house." Beginning with a cabin in the Walden woods, the "house" assumes cosmic proportions by the end of *Walden*. The "house" begins to suggest one's spiritual self. "Better paint your house your own complexion; let it turn pale or blush for you" (*Walden* 45). With the onset of certain seasons, observes Thoreau, the instinct to migrate affects not only "nations and individuals" ("Walking"), but also birds and animals. This urge to travel to new places becomes so strong that even the fear of death does not deter those undertaking migration. While birds and animals instinctually know the direction they should travel to, the humans seem to have lost this capacity to feel the "subtle magnetism in Nature" ("Walking"), which invites the walkers to proceed in certain directions. As a result, human evolution has reached stagnation not only physically but also spiritually. If walking upright is the only act that distinguishes human beings from other species, if it is a defining human act, do we cease to be humans if we shun walking? *Walden* and "Walking" answer in the affirmative. Moreover, states Thoreau, while one has to travel to the East to "realise history and study the works of art and literature" ("Walking"), one has to return to the West for material progress. Humankind should seek, to quote him, "from the East light; from the West fruit" ("Walking"). In other words, humans began their journey of progress from the East to the West. If the West symbolises material progress, the East epitomises spiritual excellence – both are thus complementary to each other. Walking back and forth is the only way to join material progress with spiritualism, the body with the soul, and science with art.

Using the insights of Laurence D. Cooper, one can more clearly understand Thoreau's understanding of the human condition. He, indeed, makes a similar observation: "Human beings and human life must be understood in the light of their having *become* (emphasis mine) what they are" (Cooper 474). The idea of the decline of human spiritual capacities is not a recent phenomenon; it can be traced to very old, even prehistoric times. The Christian myth of the

Fall is, in fact, an epoch in the quasi-mythical hi(story) of the evolution of humankind condensed into the span of a day that saw the human beings come down symbolically – reverse evolution – from Eden, the first home and the original place of grace (Buffon qtd. in Macfarlane 24).[29] Jean Jacques Rousseau, in *Second Discourse*, states that being subjected to civilised culture, human beings had to discard a great part of their original nature – he terms this loss as the second fall, the cultural fall (Skillen 107). Before the Original Fall from goodness, human virtue lay in "undeveloped innocence, as the self was not social or self-conscious" (Cooper 472). The second fall is considered worse than the first, as it has resulted in the self's alienation from itself (Rousseau 58). Like Rousseau, Thoreau emphasises humankind's twice fallen state and advocates the urgent need for a quest for wholeness and redemption – a profound inner quest, but not without strong external reverberations. Obviously, a philosopher like Thoreau did not have any other choice than walking into the woods in the quest for "gnosis," i.e. knowing through experience *and* observation (emphasis mine) (Borror 43).

Thoreau notes that "knowledge is our positive ignorance; ignorance our negative knowledge" ("Walking"). Mere factual knowledge does not help when a person walks into the woods on a quest to know the self and the world. Human hubris in regarding knowledge as possession can be dangerous, especially when one is ignorant of one's ignorance, and one's actions, on the basis of *one's* (my emphasis) knowledge, might harm others, who might have *their* (my emphasis) own version knowledge to guide their actions. This is the dilemma of the modern idea of knowledge making it subservient to the individual ego, which is liable to undergo changes.[30]

29 Georges Buffon quoted by Robert Macfarlane in *Mountains of the Mind: A History of a Fascination*. Granta, 2009. Page 24.

30 Ego (Latin: "I"), Freud posits ego as the mental agency guiding rational thinking of a personality by mediating between the outer and inner worlds. In the mind ego works as a balancing agency between the opposite drives of the id and the superego. The ego provides stability and uniformity to behaviour by providing a "personal point of reference" with the help of memory. The ego is liable to changes throughout life, especially under challenging conditions such as perception of threat, illness, and other changes having a significant bearing on it

Horkheimer and Adorno term it as "the triumph of subjectivity" (20). As a result, the idea of knowledge that is fulfilled by its "social, historical and human meaning" tends to be abandoned (20). Likewise, Thoreau wants us to develop awareness about the limits of our knowledge so as to prevent its misuse in acting out the worst fears of an individual ego. Moreover, just like nature accords an equal place to light and darkness, knowledge should give space to ignorance also. Thoreau's idea of nature includes human nature in perfect harmony with the external nature; out of this consonance is born the awareness of the impossibility of knowledge as a mere tool of the ego. To quote Thoreau, "I do not know that this higher knowledge amounts to anything more definite than a novel and grand surprise on a sudden revelation of the insufficiency of all that we called knowledge before…." ("Walking"). If "our philosophy" is a dream, we know that dreams are never fully recalled and understood. Being asleep to the call of the cock, which awakes every morning with nature, is a refusal to connect with nature, which is intelligence personified. To quote Thoreau, "Nature is a personality so vast and universal that we have never seen one of her features" ("Walking"). He conveys the same idea of the impossibility of complete knowledge with the help of an image in which a philosopher is looking at the sun to "know" it ("Walking"). Laws of natural sciences, observes Thoreau, can be transcended if one develops a relation with the "lawmaker" ("Walking"). Therefore, instead of striving to master nature, humans should respect nature and its intelligence. This humble acceptance can liberate humankind from the bondage of the notion of knowledge as a personal possession ("Walking"). The image of the sunlit meadow near the end of the essay "Walking" appears like a paradise reached, not in the physical sense, but as a transcendental awareness of higher reality. It recalls the image of the "Holy Land" at the opening of "Walking," which a walker desires to achieve. Moreover, the awakening, for Thoreau, is more of a metaphor to exemplify "individual growth" (Champion 47). It denotes the development of an awareness of light in our mind

---

See. "Ego." The Editors of Encyclopaedia, *Encyclopaedia Britannica*, 2018. URL: https://www.britannica.com/topic/ego-philosophy-and-psychology Access Date: July 07, 2020 in order to see ourselves and the world clearly. This is the vocation of the philosopher to see clearly.

It is obvious that Thoreau's chief concern in *Walden* is the making of a spiritual rather than a worldly human being (Monteiro 795). Thoreau went to the woods because he wished "to [con]front only the essential facts of life" experientially and reveal them to humanity (Thoreau 81). The way Thoreau chooses to undergo that experience has affinities with the Vedic *vanaprasthana*,[31] which is an equivalent of spiritual travel to explore the mind. At the end of two years and two months, he returns to civilised society. Why does he go there if he is to come back? Does the experiment with walking and solitary living in the woods lead to any accomplishment? Since *Walden* is an allegory of the awakening of the human soul, the answer to the first question may be glimpsed in the words of C. G. Jung on the initial signals of the process of awakening of the unconscious. He notes that when the unconscious tends to awaken (Jung 365), it puts an enormous strain on the existing psychological apparatus, which has to contain the rush of psychic energy[32] (Freud 23-25). Jung terms this stage as "confession," the cleansing of the psychological sedimentation of a lifetime that has to happen first if a person is to embrace the new dawn of the spirit. This often demands a break from social life. In most cases, there is a danger of the subject faltering when s/he faces the unconscious, and consequently, there may be regression (Jung 66). If everything proceeds correctly, the long-drawn process of the flowering of the soul takes place, and the subject can eventually return to normal life with an awakened self. So it seems to have happened in the case of Thoreau. Since he started practising walking as a spiritual practice at an early age, it can be argued that he may have experienced initial signals of awakening necessitating a break

---

31 *Varnasramadharama*, a Hindu Vedic concept, sets human life in four stages: *brahmacari-ashram,* life as a student; *Grihasta,* the married life; *Vanaprashta,* life as a recluse in the forest and *Sannyasa*, life as a wanderer who has renounced home and society. Jogiraj Basu quoted by Patrick Olivelle.

See.Olivelle, Patrick. *The Asrama System: The History and Hermeneutics of a Religious Institution*. Oxford University Press, 1993. Print.

32 Freud considers the instance of external trauma as the primary trigger in giving the first upward push to the unconscious.

See. Freud, Sigmund. *Beyond the Pleasure Principle.* Translated and edited by James Strachey, W.W. Norton & Company, 1961, pages 23-25.

from social life for some time. The answer to the second question – did the experiment with walking and solitary living in the woods lead to any accomplishment? – is also in the affirmative. During his stay at the Walden Pond, Thoreau's self begins to transform, which is reflected in his heightened awareness of himself vis-à-vis his surroundings. Moreover, on his return, Thoreau is an enlightened human being who can view his world from a new perspective. As a result, he writes one of the most insightful critiques of his contemporary civilisation in *Walden*.

Why does Thoreau choose to couch his narrative in irony, which is not so common in the solemn works of philosophy, also demands explanation? An utterance that presupposes double audience – one that shall hear and not understand all; the other that shall understand, and be amused at the former's lack of understanding, is called ironical.[33] Thoreau's use of irony in *Walden* is integrated with the organic structure of the text. Not to understand the title of *Walden* – which is an example of metaplasmus[34] (Quinn 23) on the word "world" like Godot[35] for "God," Santiago[36] for "Saint," and *Nineteen Eighty-Four*[37] for 1948 – is to miss out the subtle ironies not only in the title, but also in the whole text of which the title works as a metaphorical as well as a geographical anchorage. To speak of "the divinity in man" (Thoreau 9) to an audience deeply nurtured in the materialistic culture of early capitalism must have seemed an absurd idea to Thoreau; hence he may have decided to employ irony in *Walden* to convey the spiritual message to the readers indirectly. Like in *Gulliver's Travels*, the irony in *Walden* is so subtle and deep that, at times, the manifest meaning seems deceptively to be the only

---

33 Fowler, W. H. *Dictionary of Modern English Usage*. Oxford University Press, 2009.

34 Also called "effective misspelling" A stylistic device in which words are purposely misspelt for achieving desired aesthetic effect.

See. Quinn, Arthur. *Figures of Speech: Sixty Ways to Turn a Phrase*. Routledge, 2010.

35 A play *Waiting for Godot* by Samuel Beckett.

See. Beckett, Samuel. *Waiting for Godot: Tragicomedy in Two Acts*. Grove Press, 1954.

36 Principal character in the novel Golding, William. *Lord of the Flies: A Novel.* New York: Perigee, 2006.

37 George Orwell's dystopian novel in English written in 1948 but published in 1949. Orwell, George. 1984. London: Secker and Warburg, 1949.

meaning. Some of the ironic statements may be noted: Thoreau states that he makes it sure to be present at the sunrise though he does not assist the sun to rise in any way, and it is of "the last importance" (17) to him. The meaning of this observation veers to the opposite because to witness the sunrise is symbolic of witnessing oneself rise spiritually, and it is the first, not the last, important thing in the morning. Again, when he complains that his meetings with the gusts of wind have gone unnoticed by the newspapers, he expects the intelligent reader to understand that he considers conversing to the wind more important than reading the newspapers. Indeed, the newspapers are as indifferent to him as he is to them. To cite another example with a touch of irony in *Walden*, Thoreau notes that he spends long hours peering into the sky to catch a glimpse of a shooting star, but he never succeeds in finding one. Thoreau probably wants to suggest that the business of the world is no better than catching a shooting star. However, the philosopher is at an advantage over the world insofar as he knows that he is not going to get at anything, and he enjoys the act of watching. Apart from irony, he also makes use of allegory to knit his multi-layered narrative.

Allegory, as a way of telling a story, seems natural to the human mind. Allegory is "a figurative narrative or description, conveying a veiled moral meaning, an extended metaphor" ("Allegory"). As a rule, allegorical works have more than one meaning, i.e. they may have one or more layers of meaning over and above the obvious meaning (Fletcher 2-4). Why does Thoreau choose the form of an allegory? Maybe he thinks the modern reader might not be interested in a didactic work. To enrich his story, he might have decided to offer a parallel, interesting and easy to understand the story. On the surface level, *Walden* may be called a work belonging to the genre of transcendental literature, in which a maverick transcendentalist ("transcendentalism")[38] experiments with solitary living in the woods for two years and two months. And this is precisely how *Walden* was received by the majority of critics and reviewers at the time of its publication (Dean 293-328). But the terms like "transcendentalism"

38 An idealistic philosophical and social movement, which developed in New England around 1836 in reaction to Rationalism, and held that the Divine pervades all nature and humanity. Ralph Waldo Emerson and Henry David Thoreau were the central figures of the movement.

See: *Oxford Dictionary of English*, Third Edition, 2010.

not only impede a full and fair appreciation of the text but also tend to overshadow its richness. This happened in the case of *Walden*, as nearly all reviewers declared it a transcendentalist work. To impose a framework on a text like *Walden* can obstruct the view of a work's concreteness and singularity as a literary work rooted in a specific time and place. Though Thoreau tried to foreground *Walden* as a concrete text, so that it should be read as *Walden* only, and not as anything else. Maybe, Thoreau wants to alert the reader not to read *Walden* as a descriptive piece of nature writing only. Yet, one can also read *Walden* gainfully as an allegory of the awakening and flowering of the human soul (Monteiro 795), with walking and solitary hermitage as the two principal enabling practices. Allegory is intricately woven in the body of the text, yet Thoreau sometimes removes its veil to speak directly about the need to awaken to a new dawn of the spirit: "It appeared to me that for a like reason men (sic) remain in their present low and primitive condition; but if they should feel the influence of *spring of springs* (emphasis mine) arousing them, they would of necessity rise to a higher and more ethereal life" (Thoreau 40).

Another challenge Thoreau must have faced is finding a suitable form and language to convey the profound religio-philosophical ideas to the modern reader. The language of his age is a market-oriented language used for commodity transactions – the only language that is understood by the majority. Thoreau's predicament at the language of his age also hints at the condition of language in our times in which it has become a resource in the globalised market (Fairclough 163-64). Nevertheless, Thoreau takes up the language of his age and adapts it to his purpose. In doing so, he writes it back to the market in its language. As a result, some purely commercial terms, like "economy," "house," "fuel," "furniture," "income," "expenditure," "construction material," and "budget" assume new meanings in *Walden*, which are, at times, contrary to their market denotations. In this way, Thoreau, the philosopher, responds to the onslaught of commercialism against art and aesthetics. Rather than learning political economy, argues Thoreau, one should learn and practise life's economy, which, according to him, is synonymous with philosophy as a way of living (48). Thoreau writes *Walden* as an allegory, yet he "roots" it firmly in the time and the place. Because Thoreau does not want to pass on abstract philosophy to the reader, rather the philosophy tested on the touchstone of his felt experience. Therefore, he applies his philosophy first on himself by practising walking and living as a solitary recluse for two years and two months. Only those ideas that survive the practical test are shared with the reader. For instance, Thoreau experiments on how much time one should devote to the work for sustenance. He tests this idea by practising it himself during his stay near the Walden Pond and concludes that by working for about six weeks in a year, one can meet all the expenses for that year and yet have the rest of the time to oneself (58). In *Walden*, he shares his experiences of the music of the wind, the songs of the birds, the intoxicating sips of water at the Walden Pond, and the absorbing and soul-refreshing walks through the woods. He avers that these things cannot be bought and sold, and the "superfluities" which are bought and sold in the market are not at all required for a truly joyous living. One has to prune one's life to the very basics to experience the joy of living. Philosophy, according to Thoreau, is a way of living, not a corpus of knowledge to be "professed" and taught as a discipline in the universities. Thoreau maintains that we have enough "professors of philosophy" but few "practitioners of philosophy" (15). To quote Stein, "'to profess" is to be read sarcastically as "to pretend'" (203) because a professor who teaches philosophy to his students without ever putting it into practice himself should be called a "pretender," not a philosopher.

The practice of philosophy is quite difficult because it presupposes a life lived on the bare necessities of life. In other words, how a person is fed, warmed, clothed and sheltered decides whether s/he is a philosopher or not. After having obtained the necessities of life, remarks Thoreau, one should not crave luxuries; rather one should try to "root" oneself firmly in the earth (18). By this, he means that human beings should return to the fold of nature and strive for gaining a deep spiritual communion with it because one cannot attain the height without attaining the required depth. But people, observes Thoreau, do not search for meaningfulness despite having time – they find ways to kill time. As a result, a large number of people lead "a life of quiet desperation" (11). The most characteristic trait of wisdom, according to Thoreau, is not to do desperate things (11). Thoreau regards savages at an advantage over human beings (36) because human beings have failed to make use of the benefits of civilised life for their betterment. Instead of spending leisure on their spiritual growth, people work hard to obtain luxuries, which they think will give them inner comfort. Thoreau notes that luxuries cannot cure ennui as it is of spiritual origin. In other words, luxuries cannot offer *shantih*[39] (Eliot), the inner peace.

It is important to note that in some traditional cultures, the change of season is marked with a break in the routine of living. During such a break, pilgrimages to religious places are undertaken collectively by the people. Such excursions afford ample opportunities for the pilgrims to walk, talk and mix together as individuals quite differently from how they live and behave in their daily work routine. In other words, one can not only travel away to a distant place but also turn away in mind from his work-oriented identity for some time. Modernity has not only taken away such opportunities from our lives but also made spiritual travel more and more a personal affair; it is no longer undertaken as a part of the community as earlier. In order to make the journey comfortable, modern means of travel have eliminated not only walking but also "togetherness" from the pilgrimages.

Despite all the comforts offered by science and technology in the modern age, according to Thoreau, human beings feel spiritually stagnated. Horkheimer and Adorno suggest that the inventions of science move between the two extremes: either making human life extremely and unnecessarily comfortable or destroying it (156-57). In both ways, it is harmful to humanity. Thoreau terms the inventions of modern science as "pretty toys" (44) to amuse idle minds. They distract the attention from oneself as they capture the gaze, which should turn inwards. A person can learn either by projecting his unconscious onto the other or by turning the mind inwards, i.e., introspecting. To quote Jung, the "sun" has to turn its beam of light inwards to illumine the self (Franz 105). Unless the mind is turned

---

39 It is the spiritual peace that the narrator wistfully longs for at the end of the epical poem "The Waste Land." In the play "*Murder in the Cathedral*" by Eliot, Thomas Becket, the Archbishop dwells upon "Peace" in detail. His "Peace" is not the peace as it appears to the world. It is inner peace bestowed by the *Guru*, the Master on the disciple. See. Eliot, T. S. "The Waste Land." *Poetry Foundation*, 2020. https://www.poetryfoundation.org/poems/47311/the-waste-land

.... *Murder in the Cathedral.* Longman Study Edition, Faber and Faber, 1935, pp.56.

inwards, one is confined to learning only through projection[40] – projecting one's complexes onto others (Berenson 77)[41] instead of facing and resolving them – which might prove to be problematic for both the self and the other. Moreover, in extreme cases where one is completely unaware of its workings, one might attack the bearer of one's projected complexes – the result is more complication rather than resolution. The pitfalls of projection are convincingly brought forth in Macbeth's imagining a ghost, projecting it onto his friends, and attacking them, who are mere vehicles of his complexes (Act III, Sc II, line 13-40; Act V, Scene III, Line 10-20). He projects his worst fears onto others and assaults the mirrors of his unconscious self. Consequently, the fears return with a new object of projection as soon as the former object is destroyed. It should also be noted that unlike Hegel's dynamics of a self, locked with the other in a mutually destructive embrace (111), Thoreau's self longs for self-sufficiency. Thoreau observes that the other "distort[s] authentic self-understandings" that arise out of a true inner spiritual self. Jane Bennett also agrees, "as carriers of gossip, moralisms, prejudices, and platitudes, one's fellows pose a hazard to the robustness of individuality" (561). C.G. Jung, too, admits to the limiting constraints of society: "the social goal is attained only at the cost of a diminution of personality" (364). Freud, too, imagines civilisation as a means to hold us in check rather than a system to encourage us to follow our instincts (Thurschwell 104). Thoreau, thus, urges us to learn the art of self-introspection to explore our mind while practising walking (and, if possible solitary living) in nature so as to break free of the inhibiting influence of society that discourages radical thinkers in its own times and reverences such personalities in old times.

The basis of Thoreau's critique of his world is the premise that the human body requires to maintain the "vital heat" in it to stay alive (16). Food is required to generate vital heat, and clothing and shelter

40 Jung, C. G. "The Stages of Life." *Structure and Dynamics of the Psyche,* translated by R. F. C. Hull, edited by Herbert Read et al., vol. 8, Princeton University Press, 1975, pp. 240, 244-45.

41 Hegel states that the "other self" is the only "mirror" to see the reflection of one's "self" and it is the only way through which the self can possibly understand itself.

See. Berenson, Frances. "Hegel on Others and the Self." *Philosophy*, Vol. 57, No. 219, Jan., 1982, pp. 77-90. *JSTOR.*

are needed to preserve it. But indulging in comforts and luxuries, which are not essential for survival, disrupts the process of "elevation of mankind" (15) through spiritual growth. He observes that people travel to far-off places to earn wealth and become rich so that in later years they may keep their old and exhausted bodies sufficiently warm and await death. Thoreau satirically remarks that the luxurious living of the rich people is like creating more heat than required to be alive. In other words, people burn in the heat of passion, lust and anger; when they feel the approaching chill of death, they desperately attempt to regain warmth by eating, drinking and indulging in luxuries. As a result, too much external heat deadens their sensibilities while they are still living. Thus, by highlighting that people are leading a life of "quiet desperation" (10), Henry David Thoreau heralds a critique of modernity long before it registers its formal arrival. With human beings no longer in harmony with nature, states Thoreau, a terrible stagnation and spiritual ennui have crept into our lives, which has been widely accepted as human destiny. Thoreau states prophetically that "[m]en have become the tools of their tools" (33). He finds the contemporary way of living no less than a new form of slavery, as masses are compelled to work like bonded labourers for acquiring the things they do not actually need. They have become ignorant of their ignorance, which, Thoreau believes, hinders their personal growth. Moreover, work relations, notes Thoreau, have destroyed "manliest relations" (10) – which implies natural human relations independent of the considerations of occupation and status. Preoccupied with market-driven relations, we do not treat ourselves and our fellow beings tenderly (10). Thoreau adds, "the finest qualities of our nature, like the bloom on the fruits, can be preserved only by the most delicate handling" (10). Without tenderness in relations, according to Thoreau, the sensibility to connect with nature cannot be developed.

As a practising philosopher, Thoreau takes a radical decision to live in solitude for two years and two months in the woods and to survive on the barest possible necessities. Does he recommend the same for others? Availing himself of the prolepsis,[42] Thoreau responds that he had to take this radical step because he did not have any "mentors" (11) for guiding him in his spiritual journey. The fact

42 The anticipation and answering of a possible question of a rhetorical speech. See, *Oxford Dictionary of English*, Third Edition. 2010.

that Thoreau considers himself betrayed by the elderly of society who fail to play the role of [the] archetypal "Wise Old M[e]n" (Stein 202) for him has been the reason why he had to retreat to the woods severing all ties with society for two years and two months. Lamenting the apathetic attitude of the people of his times to the spiritual matters, Thoreau reflects that for a person in the thick of worldly affairs, the idea of "divinity in man" (11) seems to be a preposterous suggestion. As a result, people, instead of looking for opportunities for their spiritual growth, tend to find novel ways to waste their time – but not without inflicting a serious injury to the flow of eternity (11). Blind to the need of breaking free from this death-like life, remarks Thoreau, "many a poor immortal soul [that he has] met well-nigh crushed and smothered under its load, creeping down the road of life..." (9). *Walden* can thus be viewed as a philosopher's answer to the ills of the contemporary culture. It is a quest for the real self against the one constructed by a materialistic culture.

Thoreau's prescription to "root" oneself is not meant for those who are complacent in their present circumstances but for those who often catch themselves complaining about everything and feel they are unable to do anything about it. Thoreau states that he always tries to improve his present time, which he regards as the meeting point of the two eternities (19). He adds that even "the common mode of living," given all its limiting imperatives, has enough spaces for a spiritually inclined person to steer his/her life to purposefulness. He advises that the inherited "old" should be ceaselessly tried and tested by every generation in its search for the "new," which needs to be continuously reinvented. In other words, the bright possibilities of the future stand constrained by the precedents if we are not prepared to look beyond the limits set by the past. Future is born out of formlessness, not from the ruins of the past. Thoreau challenges the commonly accepted belief that nothing new is possible and that every new has already been hinted at by our predecessors as if they have "exhausted the variety and joys of life" (13). The predecessors, according to this notion, seem to have experienced all the future potentialities that the human mind can imagine. Thoreau, on the contrary, asserts that human capacity to accomplish new feats has never been measured, nor can it ever be. Thoreau urges that one should let one's life be an untried experiment and must strive to shape it in a unique and fulfilling way. Thus, *Walden* can also be regarded as a work of philosophical reflection on the art of living in the age of human-machines and machine-humans.

As mentioned above, walking and solitary living are the two enabling practices in Thoreau's spiritual and philosophical journey in the woods. Along with solitary living in the Walden woods, Thoreau practises walking conscientiously as a means to connect with nature. The practice of walking, in Thoreau, acts as a conduit between the self and the natural surroundings, which helps in self-introspection and creates a greater awareness of nature. Thoreau states, "the swiftest traveller is he that goes afoot" (53). In this sense, walking is not only an act of moving from one place to another but also an evolutionary human act, which has played an important role in our evolution as human beings. Therefore, the practice of walking becomes crucial for a person who wants to connect with nature and through nature with his inner self. Paul de Man observes that our inner nature is, in fact, an "outer event," which was "internalised" (771). Walking, thus, acts as a catalyst to bring the inner and the outer worlds together. In addition, the practice of walking helps to contextualise his experience at the Walden Pond. Walking is best practised in wild nature. Thoreau asks, "What would become of us if we walked only in a garden or a mall" ("Walking")? He observes that some sects of philosophers, instead of walking into the woods, have planted some trees in their porticos to give them an appearance of the woods. Some schools of philosophy, suggests Thoreau, have become so abstract that they are completely alienated from nature. One could call them "indoor philosophers" or, at best, "garden philosophers." Thus, *Walden* questions the abstract and theoretical assumptions of Western philosophical thought.

Not only does Thoreau uphold "absolute freedom and wildness" ("Walking") as essential qualities to preserve humankind from degradation in real life, but he also regards them as indispensable in art and literature. "All good things," opines Thoreau, "are wild and free" ("Walking"). The legend of Romulus and Remus, the founders of Rome, who were suckled by a wolf, shows that a civilisation draws strength from the wild. He, as a walker, always yearns for the wild and virgin lands and hopes that each human being would be so associated with nature that its spirit exudes from his/her persona – from such an enriched land are born the poets and philosophers of excellence. He observes that tameness of the civilised life has entered art and literature as well. So that even canonical poets, like Chaucer,

Spencer, Milton and even Shakespeare, hold wildness in check in their works. In other words, all these works depict the deeds of the civilised human beings, rather than portraying the exploits of the untamed and pre-cultural precursor that Thoreau calls the "sojourner in nature" ("Walking"). Thoreau is tacitly referring to the second fall, which Rousseau termed as "the cultural fall (Skillen 107)."[43] Like Rousseau, Thoreau also emphasises the twice fallen state of human beings and rues their complacency about their low state of being ("Walking"). Ignorant of the fact that a self-realised human being can live happily on the barest necessities, they seek to alleviate ennui with luxuries – Thoreau does not say but demonstrates this. Thus, he may be called a practising philosopher. Moreover, Thoreau does not consider the human self, nature and philosophy as separate subjects.[44] Thoreau notes that "the Evil One" ("Walking"), with one stroke, transformed wild and free humankind into submissive masses. It is from this passive acceptance and the cultural conditioning of submissiveness that he wants us to break free from if we wish to awaken. According to Thoreau, mythology, more than anything else, responds to the wildness in human nature. The East, states Thoreau, has excelled in creating mythology catering to the wild in human nature; the West (which is synonymous with the wild) is "preparing to add its fables to those of the East" ("Walking"). He prophesies that American mythology would inspire poets and philosophers in the years to come.

Along with walking and solitary living, the "house" is one of the key tropes in *Walden*. Building one's house refers to constructing one's spiritual self by reclaiming land from the wilderness. The trope of the house depicting the human soul is not unique to Thoreau. The motif of a hut or cabin, built by oneself, is a recurring motif in the Indian Sanskrit epics such as *The Ramayana* and *The Mahabharata* – *The*

---

43 Jean Jacques Rousseau, in *Second Discourse*, that civilized culture has necessitated that human beings abandon much of the wildness in their nature – he regards the renunciation as the second fall, the cultural fall.

44 Unlike in Western culture, in Indian aesthetics, there is a close relationship between the knowledge of external nature (objective knowledge), and human nature (subjective knowledge) – both omplement and fulfil each other. Thoreau wrote *Walden* under the influence of Indian Sanskrit literature especially *The Bhagavad Gita.*

See. *Schwartz, Susan L., Rasa: Performing the Divine in India, Columbia University Press, 2004.*

Bhagavad Gita (Thoreau alludes to it in *Walden)* is an episode in *The Mahabharata.* Improvement in the house/cabin signifies the accomplishment of the mind in spiritual learning. It is also noteworthy that Thoreau borrows an axe to cut the trees to get wood for constructing his cabin. The act of chopping the trees and constructing a hut is a recurring motif in various spiritual and philosophical texts, and therefore, should be interpreted accordingly (Valmiki).[45] The metaphor, thus, works on two levels: the spiritual movement and action underlie the physical act of chopping wood and building the hut/cabin. C. G. Jung makes an elaborate comparison between the house and the soul (37).[46] Gaston Bachelard comments on Thoreau's subtle employment of the image of the house in his work *The Poetics of Space.*[47] To quote him, "the house image moves in both directions: they are in us as much as we are in them (96-97)." Thus, one's house is one's spiritual self, the awareness of which develops slowly as the soul of a person begins to awaken. It is remarkable that Thoreau wants the owner to construct his own house himself because building one's house oneself leads to the development of poetic faculty as birds universally sing when they weave nests. Probably, by the end of two years and two months at the Walden Pond, Thoreau was able to construct his inner house too, which he brought along with him when he returned to society. In other words, Thoreau internalises the art of spiritual living, and when he returns, he writes his experiences in the form of a literary work

---

45 See. Valmiki. "Balakanda," *Sloka and Translation, The Ramayana.* Sarga 1, IIT Kanpur, nd. Web. Accessed on 28 Aug. 2020 at 9 am.

https://www.valmiki.iitk.ac.in/sloka?field_kanda_tid=1&language=dv&field_sarga_value=1

46 C. G. Jung quoted by Gaston Bachelard in Introduction. *The Poetics of Space: The Classic Look at How We Experience Intimate Places.* By Gaston Bachelard, Translated by Maria Jolas, Beacon Press, 1964, page 37.

47 In *The Poetics of Space,* Gaston Bachelard, the French philosopher psychologically examines the spaces as an intimate part of us. He terms the method as "topoanalysis."

See. Bachelard, Gaston. Introduction. *The Poetics of Space: The Classic Look at How We Experience Intimate Places.* By Gaston Bachelard, Translated by Maria Jolas, Beacon Press, 1964, page 37.

Also See. Ellen. "Gaston Bachelard: The Poetics of Space," *The Examined Life,* 2020. Web., https://www.theexaminedlife.org/library/poetics-of-space/, Accessed on 20 Aug. 2020 at 11 am.

for humanity. In other words, he dons the role of the archetypal "wise old man" (Stein 202) to guide anyone who wishes to follow in his footsteps.

To conclude, *Walden*, in addition to being a transcendental text – which is also an allegory tempered with satiric irony – is a work deeply embedded in its time and place. The practices of walking and solitary living help it become a deeply rooted work. Moreover, walking in the wild nature, as exemplified in *Walden,* can be employed as a practice to test one's ideas on the touchstone of one's felt experience before accepting them as wisdom. In terms of being a spiritual-cum-philosophical work putting forth abstract philosophical ideas as the felt experience of the writer in the form of allegory with the elements of irony in it, *Walden* stands as a unique text in the literature of walking.

CHAPTER 3

Walking as a Motif and Act: Charles Dickens' *The Uncommercial Traveller*

> So much of my travelling is done on foot, that if I cherished betting propensities, I should probably be found registered in sporting newspapers, under some such title as the Elastic Novice, challenging all eleven-stone mankind to competition in walking.
>
> (*The Uncommercial Traveller*, Dickens 137)

> I can't express how much I want these [streets]. It seems THEY supplied something to my brain, which I cannot bear, when busy, to lose.
>
> (Dickens qtd. in Hollington 71)

This chapter examines Charles Dickens' *The Uncommercial Traveller* (1860), published as periodical papers in the magazine *All the Year Round* in the 1860s. I argue that with all the staple features of the literature of walking, Dickens' *The Uncommercial Traveller* can be placed at the threshold of the hi(story) of the literature of walking after J. J. Rousseau's *Reveries* and H. D. Thoreau's *Walden* and "Walking," and that Dickens' particular contribution lies in the fact that with him the walking writer starts contemplating his "self" in the living context of his society and times – Rousseau and Thoreau both had to walk away from society to meditate on their "self" in solitude. Since the uncommercial papers depict the narrator as a walker who walks around a place to see and understand it from a walker's perspective, and who walks at length to understand it and think about it deeply before he finally writes down the knowledge so gathered, it would be significant to examine it as an important work belonging to the literature of walking. The chapter also focuses on Dickens' fashioning of the first-person style of narration coupled with the way of journalistic reporting on social, familial and economic issues during the Victorian era of the 1860s. This combination of journalistic style and literary acumen for observing a place and writing about it lends the uncommercial papers a great deal of credibility for the reader and allows the writer to speak about a plethora of issues along with the main story.

It is noteworthy that the previous research on Dickens' *The Uncommercial Traveller* considers some crucial aspects of his approach to journalism, i.e. first-person narration, personal and confidential stance with the readers, use of literary and rhetorical language, instead of factual and informative language used in journalistic reporting etc. John Drew's work is foundational in terms of offering critical insights into the essays of *The Uncommercial Traveller* with reference to contemporary issues. Besides, John Drew explores the unique narrative persona employed by Dickens, an uncommercial travel-writer in an age embracing commercialism in all walks of life. This chapter begins where Drew's work ends, i.e. in this chapter, I propose to analyse *The Uncommercial Traveller* with a particular reference to the narrator's practice of walking not only as a physical activity to reach his destination, and the use of walking as a cradle for thinking about self and the world, but also the employment of walking and thinking as a literary motif in his papers. The narrator not only practises bipedal walking to gather a sense of the place but he also employs walking as a literary motif in his stories to achieve multiple objectives such as to mix up narrative points of view, to move from one issue to another, to combine various streams of thought with personal anecdotes and, also, to blend local folklore with the realistic journalistic narration.

The Uncommercial Traveller follows "a line of business," i.e. he does not wander aimlessly like a flâneur; rather, he travels to reach the destination for a particular purpose. He is commercial insofar as writing and publishing is part of commerce, and he is uncommercial because he does not belong to a privileged business house whose commercial travel agents are offered special amenities and privileges by hotels and restaurants. He travels by public transportation, stays and eats at roadside resorts and practises walking to experience the place of his interest. The title *The Uncommercial Traveller* is suggestive of the writer's concern about the onslaught of commercial and utilitarian values against the spirit of literature and culture in the Victorian era. Literature, the narrator suggests, should be commercial insofar as it is part of the publishing industry, the process of which begins when making of a literary work, as a work of art, is complete. But the making of the work of art itself should not be dictated by commercial interests. It is the beginning of such a trend in the Victorian social fabric, of which literature is a part, against which Dickens seems to be protesting in *The Uncommercial Traveller*.

Charles Dickens walks with a purpose to trace the story he is looking for, to meet the characters of the story and let the story weave itself before he writes it down for his magazine. *The Uncommercial Traveller* marks a change in the writing career of Dickens because as an Uncommercial Traveller, he cannot pen a story like a novelist without assigning a name, place and time to it and keep himself outside the action like an omniscient author with his fingers paired. Rather he walks to the place where a story is developing, he acclimatises himself with the scenario, converses with the characters while he himself being the catalyst to let the scene, characters and plot come together to form a wholesome story. Since he has to sell his stories, he makes them engagingly realistic by himself being the eyewitness, the narrator and the commentator. This makes Dickens' role larger than that of a writer; he is a writer as well as a character and a cameraman. Hazel Mackenzie observes that Dickens's *The Uncommercial Traveller* "traces the relationship between Dickens's use of the personal, his concept of the 'Uncommercial' in the series and his preoccupation with the forces of commercialism and utilitarianism, which it reads as ultimately concerned with his own sense of complicity in the commercialisation of literature" (Abstract ii). But at the core of Dickens endeavour, argues Mackenzie, one can infer that Dickens works towards opposing the fragmentation of Victorian society caused by the dehumanising tide of commercialism and utilitarianism through his essays that embody human values such as sympathy, innocence, charity, goodwill etc. (31). Andrews also remarks that "Dickens's lifelong theme as a writer was connection, the reuniting, as in a family, of a fragmenting society, and the mitigation of the harsher effects of social and economic divisions." (21). The difference between a preacher and the Uncommercial Traveller lies in the fact that the former preaches abstract moral platitudes from the pulpit; the latter undergo the pains to travel to certain places to experience the embodied version of the story woven with its localised time and place. The Uncommercial Traveller is thus practising what the preacher preaches.

Why does Dickens choose the medium of periodical essay over the novel of which he was a masterful writer, and why does he don the role of a "journalist" and call himself "uncommercial" when journalism is the consumerist form of writing? The answer to these questions underscores the fact that both literature and journalism were affected by the corrupting influence of consumerism, so that there was hardly any space left in them for Dickens to achieve his objective. Literature was talked of disparagingly as "imaginative writing," and journalism was meant for the readers' everyday consumption. In other words, readers approach literature, especially novels, with the pre-conceived notion that the writer is writing "creatively" not "reporting" factual news, whereas a journalist is thought of as reporting facts dispassionately from the ground situation in matter-of-fact language. Dickens as Uncommercial Traveller hybridises literary writing and journalistic reporting. He pours out his felt experiences in a poignantly poetic language and reports them in the style of a journalist. In other words, Dickens' walk is poised between the monotonous reporting language of a journalist and the literary language of a novelist capable of transferring the felt experiences to the reader. Additionally, he adds to his tool kit the first-hand investigation of an inspector at the place of happening. With such a combination of diverse tools, Dickens is able to forge an experiential story that is not "narrated" but "reported" by the "reporter" right from the theatre of life through the medium of poetic prose.

As mentioned earlier, *The Uncommercial Traveller* not only reports from the place out there but also tempers his realistic narrative with his deepest nostalgic musings. For example, the Uncommercial Traveller feels dismayed to witness that the old historical buildings are being erased to construct citadels of trade and commerce, countless trees are being felled to make way for the expanding roads, and big complexes are usurping open grounds because he would miss certain places where he had played as a child. The Uncommercial Traveller is haunted by the memories associated with those places and buildings and feels that with the geographical changes in a place, a parallel psychological trauma is caused to the people who have a deep association with those places, and their next generations would be devoid of those places forever. While reading the pages of *The Uncommercial Traveller*, one does not feel lachrymose at all; rather, one feels a personal touch that is subtly employed by the writer to evoke the reader's own memories of the places, of which the reader might be conscious as well. Such a personal bond with the reader is a singular achievement of *The Uncommercial Traveller*, which makes it stand apart from a mere journalistic report. The Uncommercial Traveller has thus been successful in implanting literary "DNA" to his stories that would otherwise have appeared journalistic/historical reporting with no enduring value.

The narrative persona of the Uncommercial Traveller also keeps a fluid identity. Sometimes he steps into the shoes of the character, real or imaginary, and narrates the character from his perspective. Sometimes he captures and relates the felt experience of the subject from various points of view. Victor Fournel terms Dickens' persona *badaud*, i.e. someone who had no identity of his own but an airy persona that can enter into any mind and speaks on its behalf (qtd. in Daniel Tyler 14) – also, this airy garb is donned by the author at times to assume omniscience, at times, to reminisce his dear past, which is why some parts of the text of *The Uncommercial Traveller* reads like an autobiographical journey down the "memory lanes" – through which he walks – literally. Hazel Mackenzie also makes a similar observation: "The figure of the Uncommercial Traveller (sic) vacillates between a fully realised human agent and an anonymous representative, an observer whose personality is subsumed in the act of observing" (31). However, due to the complex nature of the narrative persona of *The Uncommercial Traveller,* Hazel Mackenzie cautions us to read the text as a psychological autobiography of Charles Dickens: "…the adoption of a persona and the particular use that Dickens makes of it puts into question the autobiographical readings that the texts invite…'The Uncommercial Traveller' (sic) introduces an element of doubt into the mix, by telling a very personal story about the paralysing effects of impersonality in commerce, in literature, and in society in general" (32-33). John Drew shares a similar view about the elusive narrative persona that Dickens employs in *The Uncommercial Traveller,*

> Dickens modulates almost imperceptibly between making what are effectively authorial statements to the reader, and recording the thoughts of his persona within a narrative framework, and the essay therefore illustrates the close but never reliable correspondence between the two which gives The Uncommercial Traveller (sic) its characteristic literary nuance. The result is a curious mixture of representation which has both factual and fictional traits, of rhetoric and narrative, but which nevertheless proves satisfactory because of its approximation to the reader's private experience of the interactive relationship between thought and action. (228)

On the other side, adds Drew, Dickens' narratorial acrobatics do compromise objectivity in the narrative. To quote, "…sheer variety of tone and narrative stance precludes the projection of a single personality, and at the same time often prejudices [Dickens'] ability to appear objective (Drew 149). It can be argued that what is considered a fault in realistic fiction is regarded an accomplishment in the literature of walking to which Dickens uncommercial papers belong; and that neither it was Dickens' aim to sound objective nor would it suit the needs of the genre he was pioneering while working on the essays for his magazine.

John Drew remarks that Butor's theoretical insights with respect to "iterology" and Baudelaire's and Benjamin's theory and practice of flânerie exemplified in *The Flowers of Evil* (1993); and *The Arcades Project* (2002) respectively can provide crucial theoretical co-ordinates to appreciate *The Uncommercial Traveller* whose walks earn him the status of a flâneur in the mid-Victorian city (172). When Dickens' approach in *The Uncommercial Traveller* is compared with those of Baudelaire's and Benjamin's, one can notice certain similarities as well as differences in their approaches. At about the time when Dickens was undertaking these supposedly purposeful walks, Baudelaire was engaged with the idea of flâneur, a modern city stroller in France who walks for the sake of the experience of walking (Baudelaire 9). However, as pointed out by Victor Fournel, the narrative persona in *Uncommercial Traveller* is more versatile in its approach than what flâneur can afford. Victor Fournel observes, "simple *flâneur* is always in possession of his individuality whereas the individuality of *badaud* disappears" (qtd. in Daniel Tyler 14). Thus, it is easy to infer that though Baudelaire's flâneur loves to be amidst the masses incognito, it does not mean he sheds his identity altogether. Instead, he does not change externally, but he orientates himself spiritually to become a "child" who experiences everything with child-like wonder. He does not slough off his identity altogether as *Badaud* does, but he does assume a narratorial perspectival position (sheds "I" to embrace "we") so as to mix in the crowd. This is precisely what the *Badaud* does. Walter Benjamin notes that "The social base of flânerie is journalism. As flâneur, the literary man ventures into the marketplace to sell himself" (*The Arcades Project*, Benjamin 446). Thus, it can be argued that Dickens and Baudelaire were unknowingly working on analogous ideas at about the same historical period. However, it should be noted that flâneur was one of "the devices of journalism" before it was formally adopted as the prototype of a practising thinker in a modern city (448).

Tyler further writes that Dickens' narrative persona of The *Uncommercial Traveller* is a descendent of the semi-autobiographical narrator of periodicals such as *The Spectator*, *The Idler*, *The Rambler* and others (13). Therefore, it is more versatile than flâneur. At times, the narrator becomes critical and censoring like a sanitation inspector, for instance, when he happens to visit an eatery for the working classes in the essay "The Boiled Beef of New England"; sometimes, he holds back his personality altogether and focuses on journalistic reporting as for example in the essay "The Shipwreck;" at times, he chooses to mingle so completely with the crowd that he becomes indistinguishable from it, as for example in the essay "Two Views of a Cheap Theatre" when Dickens takes the point of view of the audience: "We were a motley assemblage of people, and we had a good many boys and young men among us; we had also many girls and young women." (Dickens 88)

Charles Dickens, as the writer of *The Uncommercial Traveller,* may be considered a flâneur because his methodology was identical to the flâneur as imagined by Baudelaire. In it, Dickens has combined the abstract motif of life as travel, during which the traveller, with the act of travelling/walking to a destination, meeting people and seeing places on the way, leaves his memories and traces behind to be read by those who come retracing his footsteps. It is a record of narrator's – who is a disguised voice of the author himself – walk around a number of locations such as workhouses, theatres and churches, factories, alms-houses in London. Besides London, the "Uncommercial Traveller" visits Liverpool twice to have a look at the docks; he travels to the city of Rochester where he had spent his childhood, to the dockyard at Chatham, England, to Italy and twice to France where he visits the mortuary. The essays document the Victorian way of social observation and articulation (Chris R. 523).

The essay entitled "Poor Mercantile Jack" records his night wanderings as a member of a police squad hunting for the swindlers who have laid traps for 'poor Jack.' There is a clever play of narratorial point of view between the general and the particular as sometimes Jack seems to be a particular person, sometimes a general representation of a sailor. Just like his aimless rambles, especially the present one during the night, Dickens is searching for the person as well as the point of view from which to narrate his story. In the essay "Wapping Workhouse," Dickens states his peculiar style of wandering, "having lost my way, and, abandoning myself to the narrow streets in a Turkish frame of mind, relied on predestination to bring me somehow or other to the place I wanted, if I were ever to get there" (25)? W.G. Sebald's approach to walking is similar to Dickens' because both like to walk to a place in an unplanned way. To quote, "If you look at a dog following the advice of his nose, he traverses a patch of land in a completely unplottable manner. And he invariably finds what he's looking for. I think that, as I've always had dogs, I've learned from them how to do this" (Sebald, "Conversation" 94).

Though the Uncommercial Traveller travels great distances by the available means of transportation, he prefers walking at the site of the story. "The Shipwreck" narrates the touching story of the drowning of the Royal Charter off the coast at Llanalgo in Anglesey, which went down with five hundred human beings on board. The Uncommercial Traveller pays a visit to the scene of the wreck and the churchyard where over one hundred and forty-five bodies were kept, identified, and ceremonially buried by the local clergyman and his family consisting of his wife and his sister-in-law. In "The Ship Wreck," the Uncommercial Traveller wished to bring to limelight the humanitarian concern of the clergyman and his family for performing the last burial rites of one hundred and forty-five dead strangers. The Uncommercial Traveller takes a particular interest in "reading" the signs on the site he visits before he writes about it (Butor 162); writing cannot happen without learning the art of walking and reading – faces, books, landscape, seascape and so on. Butor further notes that the Uncommercial Traveller walks between the graveyard and the room that was the makeshift mortuary and the house of the clergyman where he lived with his family; The Uncommercial Traveller even dines with the clergyman and his family. Walking thus enables the Uncommercial Traveller not only observe the place minutely but also feel the invisible presences which can only be sensed, and, which were, then, to be articulated by Dickens. Mark how like a skilled navigator the Uncommercial Traveller observed the site where the ship had sunk:

> The tide was on the flow, and had been for some two hours and a half; there was a slight obstruction in the sea within a few yards of my feet: as if the stump of a tree, with earth enough about it to keep it from lying horizontally on the water, had slipped a little from the land – and as I stood upon the beach and observed it dimpling the light swell, that was coming in, I cast a stone over it. (3)

It was during those walking and sensing journeys between the places that his mind could form the thoughts lucidly which he would write down on paper at the end of the day: "It was some time before I could sever myself from the many interesting papers on the table, and then I broke bread and drank wine with the kind family before I left them" (21).

It will be a grave mistake if we overlook the clergyman who was the first walker, reader, writer and teller of the story of the wreck. It was the clergyman who walked to the site where the bodies were lying and took many rounds between these places. It can be argued that he wrote the story of the wreck on the land with his footprints and, then, the Uncommercial Traveller was one of the many "pilgrims" who would "walk" to "read" and reminisce the history after reading it in the magazine *All the Year Round.* The Uncommercial Traveller drops a hint for the reader: "It was the clergyman himself from whom I heard this, while I stood on the shore, looking in his kind wholesome face as it turned to the spot where the boat had been" (6). To quote Butor's words in slightly altered context, "The surface of the earth becomes a page and an imprint is left upon it. Wandering, then, is staked out signs, with characters" (6). It was the clergyman who "read the marks" and "marked the sites" – "tomb is a mark *par excellence...*" (Butor 6). Even the Uncommercial Traveller is moved by the clergyman's efforts in "reading" the bodies of the dead for any signs, which would, later on, be referred to the family members for identification. As a result, many bodies were exhumed and then re-buried by the relatives after identification: "Several bodies had been exhumed from the graves of four, as relatives had come from a distance and seen his register; and, when recognised, these have been re-buried (sic) in private graves, so that the mourners might erect separate headstones over the remains" (Dickens 12). Thus, the Uncommercial Traveller expects the reader to "read" the "register," i.e. the style of language of the narrator, just like the mourners read the register of records prepared by the clergyman and, then, identified their dear ones. As a general note, the Uncommercial Traveller also wants to suggest that we are all relatives of each other as we are all human beings, and so should we identify ourselves.

One has to notice the "register" of the narrator's account in the essay "The Shipwreck." In keeping with his purpose of travelling/walking for the house of "Human Interest Brothers," i.e. travelling/walking in search of human beings engaged in the service of humanity selflessly (Drew 190), the register of the narrator's language conveys humanitarian concern through subtle yet effective touches. A plain journalist would have reported that the ship sank with five thousand people on board. But mark the register of the Uncommercial Traveller, "[She] went down with her treasure of at least five hundred human lives" (Dickens 5). The ship was carrying gold in good quantities, which was "surely and steadily coming up" (7), but for the narrator, the real "treasure" was not gold but "five hundred human lives" with which the Royal Charter went down. One can find numerous examples of Dickens' use of literary/figurative devices to convey much more than mere journalistic prose. John Drew dwells on the Uncommercial Traveller's humanitarian intentions in the self-introduction at the outset. "I travel, notes the narrator, for the great house of Human Interest Brothers, and have rather a large connexion in the fancy goods way" (2). Drew interprets "Human Interest Brothers" as the Uncommercial Traveller's interest in humanity and humanitarian concerns, which would obviously be "uncommercial." But he has, adds Drew, a connection to "selling" and "fancy goods" which means the use of literary resources to "amuse and instruct" (Drew 191) and his "goods" – unlike a commercial traveller's curious commodities – are the essays which would be on sale as periodical papers.

As mentioned earlier, it is customary for the Uncommercial Traveller to practise walking to get a sense of the place he visits in search of a story. When the Uncommercial Traveller leaves for the Wapping Workhouse, he seems to be in no hurry to get there, instead, he lingers around for a while; it is by no means a straight walk to the destination with no waste of time. Dickens' credo of walking is not transportational only, i.e. for reaching the desired place as quickly as possible. To quote, "Long before I reached Wapping, I gave myself up as having lost my way, and abandoning myself to the narrow streets in a Turkish frame of mind, relied on predestination to bring me somehow or other to the place I wanted if I were ever to get there" (Dickens 25). Transportational walking might also be called proletarian walking because a city worker has to reach the factory in a given time. In this sense, artistic walking, which Dickens practises, is a self-reflexive activity. And by virtue of being as such, artistic walking poses a challenge to the founding principles of commodification and consequent reification[48] under capitalism. It is the singular triumph of Dickens art in *The Uncommercial Traveller* that he uses the platform of capitalism to resist its onslaught at Victorian art, literature and culture.

The essay "Wapping Workhouse" opens with the Uncommercial Traveller warming up his spirits with some walking, to see and think and, thus, to establish a spiritual connection with the place. As the Uncommercial Traveller is walking through the lanes, identifying the landmarks on the way and recalling the literary figures associated with them, they too seem to be responding to him. In other words, he seems to be talking, not only with the inanimate object as he walks past, but also "talks" with the "past." Note the walking and thinking monologue at the beginning of the essay "Wapping Workhouse:"

My day's no-business beckoning me to the East end of London, I had turned my face to that point of the metropolitan compass on leaving Covent Garden, and had got past the India House, thinking in my idle manner of Tippoo-Sahib and-Charles Lamb, and had got past my little wooden midshipman, after affectionately patting him on one leg of his knee-shorts for old acquaintance' sake, and had got past Aldgate Pump, and had got past the Saracen's Head (with an ignominious rash of posting-bills disfiguring his swarthy countenance), and had strolled up the empty yard of his ancient neighbour the Black or Blue Boar, or Bull, who departed this life I don't know when, and whose coaches are all gone I don't know where; and I had come out again into the age of railways, and I had got past Whitechapel Church, and was-rather inappropriately for an Uncommercial Traveller-in the Commercial Road. Pleasantly wallowing in the abundant mud of that thoroughfare, and greatly enjoying the huge piles of building belonging to the sugar refiners, the little masts and vanes in small back gardens in back streets, the neighbouring canals and docks, the India-vans lumbering along their stone tramway, and the pawnbrokers' shops where hard-up Mates had pawned so many sextants and quadrants, that I should have bought a

48 When the worker becomes a factor in the production process and the social relations based on the economic base are treated (reified) as natural.

See. "reification." *Oxford Reference. Oxford University Press.* Date of access 28 Jun. 2021,
https://www.oxfordreference.com/view/10.1093/oi/authority.20110803100412880

few cheap if I had the least notion how to use them, I at last began to file off to the right, towards Wapping.... in the streets of a city where every stone seemed to call to me, as I walked along," this way, man, and see what waits to be done!" (Dickens 23-38)

John Drew has mentioned some literary and historical details of the landmarks identified by the Uncommercial Traveller while walking on the way to the Wapping Workhouse (265-266). If one carefully reads the above walking monologue, one can infer how effortlessly the Uncommercial Traveller can walk back and forth several dimensions that his surroundings have to offer, peep through the present back into the past and associate objects and persons held apart in space and time.

The Uncommercial Traveller thus practises walking to "read" the footprints of the "past" on the paths passing through the "present." Walking and thinking is thus the primary ritual that precedes reading, seeing and spiritually connecting with the place the Uncommercial Traveller intends to visit; the writing seems to be the concluding process of weaving the bits of experiences so collected into the threads of sentences expressing patterns of felt thoughts. The reader would re-perform the psychological walk through the lanes of felt thoughts but with the narrator as a guide.

When Drew observes that "the essay [Wapping Workhouse] is a good example of Dickens' efforts at handling, if not resolving, social problems through a representation of thought modified by action" (264), he oversimplifies the process of walking and experiential thinking in one phrase "thought modified by action." One can see that walking and thinking begins even before the Uncommercial Traveller reaches the intended destination and continues even after he leaves the place. It can be argued that reporting about the Workhouse becomes incidental to a stroll in the city. He went to Workhouse because it fell on the way, and being a journalist sensitive human suffering, he could not go past it without documenting the miserable condition of the inhabitants of the Workhouse. Thus, it can further be argued that the purpose was to "walk and think" not to reach a geographical destination as a finality but only as a temporary stopover for a traveller who travels across the lanes of time. Yet from a journalistic/realistic perspective, the Uncommercial Traveller walks to the "Wapping Workhouse" to inspect the wards in which lunatic women were leading a miserable life, and, to relate their story in the magazine *All the Year Round.* The Uncommercial Traveller had read a report about the miserable condition of the lunatic women at the Wapping Workhouse in the local newspaper in which the city magistrate had expressed outrage at the inhuman treatment being meted out to the mentally sick people. Dickens goes to the Wapping Workhouse "to see" (24) how "facts" about "Wapping Workhouse" reported in the newspapers stood to reality – the lost link between the newspapers that reports does not narrate, and the literature that narrates without reporting. In other words, the need of the hour is a genre that combines newspaper reporting with literature. The reader can read it like a newspaper and feel it like a novel. In an age when literature is dismissed as fiction, and journalistic writing is regarded dull, Dickens' *The Uncommercial Traveller* shows the way. It can be remarked that Dickens fulfils the gap between journalistic reporting and literature by combining the best in the two genres.

Accompanied by the Workhouse matron, the Uncommercial Traveller walks and narrates what he sees inside the "Foul Wards" where everybody except the Workhouse warden has fits of madness, epilepsy, hysteria and so on. There were infants too in the Workhouse whose cries made the Uncommercial Traveller wonder whether it was "pleasant or painful" for children to be at such a hopeless place (30). Then the Uncommercial Traveller walks through "the Refractories" where inhabitants who were picking oakum all the time, were invariably infected with ailments of tonsils and uvula due to the nature of their work. While those who were working seemed to have lost all hope in God, others who were frail and bedridden evinced a great faith in His ways. When the matron had no more wards to show, the journey to the Workhouse stood completed, the Uncommercial Traveller muses that such wards "ought not to exist; no person of common decency and humanity can see them and doubt it" (37).

The opening of the essay "Two Views of a Cheap Theatre" establishes the mood of the narrator as well the sets the tone for the essay. The word images such as "desolate…Covent-garden," "dreadfully low-spirited" and "damp" painted by the narrator anticipate the hopeless state in which the institution of theatre has gotten itself. The statue of Shakespeare represents the apotheosis in which the drama in England had been at that time, and the drop of rainwater oozing from the nose of the statue of Shakespeare (the drops of rainwater fall short of tears of dejection from Shakespeare's eyes) reinforces the idea of dampness inflicting spirit of the theatre

Shakespeare had bequeathed to England. Speaking on the title, one of the two views of a theatre is that primarily the theatre has to be a medium of entertainment, which was perfected by Shakespeare under whose statue the famous Drury Lane is lying in shambles. The second view is that the theatre seems "cheap" to the Uncommercial Traveller – because otherwise, it was by no means cheap (Drew 270) – is forcibly making it a medium of evangelical peaching/instruction. The following lines carry forward the same mood of desolation in connotative as well as denotative sense.

> Those wonderful houses about Drury-lane Theatre, which in the palmy days of theatres were prosperous and long-settled places of business, and which now change hands every week, but never change their character of being divided and subdivided on the ground floor into mouldy dens of shops where an orange and half a dozen nuts, or a pomatum-pot (sic); one cake of fancy soap, and a cigar-box, are offered for sale and never sold, were most ruefully contemplated that evening, by the statue of Shakespeare, with the rain-drops coursing one another down its innocent nose. (40-41)

The purpose of the Uncommercial Traveller's visit to the theatre was to compare the above two views of the theatre. However, he notes, "… its object was to compare the play on Saturday evening, with the preaching in the same Theatre on Sunday evening" (48).

Is Dickens suggesting the imminent demise of the institution of theatre? Or is he suggesting that it is being usurped by moralistic preaching, which neither the preacher know nor the audience practises – though the speaker zealously spoke to the audience, which was quite attentive to the lecture? The church personage stands in sharp contrast with the clergyman in the essay "The Shipwreck," who practises Christianity instead of preaching it to the audience in a theatre where one comes for light entertainment. The church, not the theatre, is the proper place to hear a clergyman preach. Even the plays staged in the theatre were didactic in content and presentation. Since the Uncommercial Traveller's trips are undertaken to "look on" (43), he describes the place minutely. He lets his eye hover over the place, and he paints the image in rich language. Unlike Baudelaire, whose flâneur is in search of aesthetic beauty without any immediate purpose, Dickens' narrator undertakes walks for a particular purpose of seeing a particular place which is pre-decided, and to which a particular journey is aimed. In this essay, the narrator seems to be focusing more on the art and architecture of the theatre building, probably because he is referring to the theatre building as a metaphor for the institution of theatre in England – whose sole "architect" was Shakespeare, who designed it to perfection. The narrator is relieved that the building is well ventilated and spacious, which is suggestive of the artistic freedom that the medium of drama once had. The narrator is suggesting that the genre of performative drama is not even allowed as much creative freedom as is implied in the structure of the building. However, the "object" of his journey was the spectators of the theatre, not the building. Dickens credits one person for designing the building to perfection. The meaning lies in the heart of the metaphor. Dickens finds sitting in the theatre "a motley assemblage of people" (54). As the concluding note, what can be more ironic than the presentation of pantomime on "the Spirit of Liberty" in a theatre reeling under the pressure of didacticism by the church?

The trip to theatre gives Dickens an opportunity to evaluate the relevance of the institution of theatre as means of aesthetic pleasure and moral upliftment through the representation of beauty and truth on the stage. Though the building is airy, yet the stuff on the stage is "suffocating," where the Uncommercial Traveller finds more of preaching less of drama. The reality of the "motley of people sitting in the theatre does not find reflection on the stage. Rather a personage hogs the stage to lecture to the audience on the virtue that he himself seems to have never practised. The medium of the theatre was being undermined by a speaker who could not even communicate effectively due to a lack of focus and a strange accent. The Uncommercial Traveller finds him guilty of both guilty of "spiritual vanity" and the use of "slangs and twangs" in a ceremonial address (52). For the Uncommercial Traveller, the preacher cuts a sorry figure in the address. He wonders: "In the New Testament there is the most beautiful and affecting history conceivable by man, and there are the terse models for all prayer and for all preaching. As to the models, imitate them, Sunday preachers – else why are they there, consider!" (55).

The essay "Poor Mercantile Jack" describes the Uncommercial Traveller's experience of accompanying the police team patrolling the Liverpool quayside areas during the night to check crime. The opening of the essay alludes to *Macbeth* and presiding deities of the night in Shakespearean style to build an atmosphere of surrealism, which seems to be deftly employed by the writer to avoid touching the reality of the Victorian underworld directly (Drew 279). The narrator wonders who is in charge of the affairs of the denizens at the dockyards. The good angels seem to be conspicuous by their absence and Brig. Beelzebub seems to be the guiding force for the "infernal craft" (57). In keeping with the narrative style and diction of the essay, the eponymous character Poor Mercantile Jack is also an imaginary "everyman" of the medieval Morality Plays. The writer seems to be searching for the character as well as for the language, and, also, for the point of view from which to narrate his story to the Victorian readers. Drew observes that Dickens describes squalor and prostitution at the Liverpool dockyard in the euphuistic language (279).

In the essay "Refreshments for Travellers," the Uncommercial Traveller shares with the reader his dissatisfaction with the food he is served on the way. Since he travels by railroad and he is not a commercial traveller, he has to face the cold indifference of the staff at British railway station eateries because they do not have "a pecuniary interest" in his arrival (Dickens 78). To travel as an Uncommercial traveller, the narrator rues, is not at all easy because the rise of commercialism in England in the 1860s has made uncommercial travelling, which once was the order of life, very difficult. Drew adds that since the British Railway eateries in the 1860s were let out on a contract basis, and they were interested only in those customers from whom they expected more money. The Uncommercial Traveller complains that he is yet to find a place where he "could get anything good to eat and drink in five minutes, or...was received with a welcome" (Dickens 76). In the essay, the narrator explores the loss of human touch in the dealing of the hotels and eateries catering to the travellers. With the onset of commercialism in England of 1860s, the catering businesses prefer wholesale dealing with customers in large numbers under contracts with commercial companies. The retail dealing, which Dickens suggests is more personal and human-centred because it happens on face-to-face, is more humane in its approach. Therefore, hotels expect and welcome customers who already have a contract with them (Drew 215-17). The Uncommercial Traveller sums up his views on wholesale dealings, which has replaced the retail transactions with a personal touch. To quote,

> We all know, on the other hand, the great station hotel belonging to the company of proprietors, which has suddenly sprung up in the back outskirts of any place we like to name...where nobody is glad to see us, or sorry to see us, or minds (our bill paid) whether we come or go, or

> how, or when, or why, or cares about us. We all know this hotel, where we have no individuality, but put ourselves into the general post, as it were, and are sorted and disposed of according to our division. We all know that we can get on very well indeed at such a place, but still not perfectly well; and this may be, because the place is largely wholesale, and there is a lingering personal retail interest within us that asks to be satisfied (88).

In the essay "The German Chariot," one finds the Uncommercial Traveller travelling through France, Switzerland and England. The unconscious weighs more heavily on his mind's eye than the conscious mind, and therefore, he describes certain objects as "dark objects" because he perceives them through the unconscious mind. It is not that he cannot name them, but he does not name them like other objects and situations he describes purposefully to create an eerie effect. The essay reads like a travel through the dark recesses of the unconscious mind and meeting with shadowy memories and images. John Drew terms it as "retrospective reverie" on travelling by coach. When John Drew terms Dickens as a "narrator of the moving pictures" (105-106) he misses on the metaphor of the chariot for imagination and the images from memory as physical images. In other words, Dickens is letting his mind walk through the memory lanes and lets his pen describe hurriedly what the soul's eye registers. Dickens's approach can be compared to the celebrated painter mentioned by Charles Baudelaire in *The Painter of Modern Life*, Constantin Guys, who works on his canvass feverishly lest an image should give a slip to the brush.

"The Great Tasmania's Cargo" records the Uncommercial Traveller's thoughts when he revisits the port at Liverpool where he had searched for the Poor Mercantile Jack. The narrator observes, "I had got back to that rich and beautiful port where I had looked after Mercantile Jack, and I was walking up a hill there, on a wild March morning" (108). This time the narrator goes there to have a look at the soldiers who have been discharged from the British Army, who are being brought back from India and describes their wretched condition when they were returning home. They were treated not like human beings but as "cargo." To the Uncommercial Traveller's surprise, they were being served rotten food while on board for several weeks, and many of them had died due to prolonged malnourishment. The person in charge of their well-being asserts that they were given the "best of all possible" food and amenities. The repetition of "best of all possible" is intended to emphasise the official cruelty in treating the discharged soldiers, and an obstinate official denial even to own up to a visitor the obvious institutional failure. "My hand and my heart fail me," the Uncommercial Traveller writes, "in writing my record of this journey. The spectacle of the soldiers in the hospital-beds of that Liverpool workhouse (a very good workhouse, indeed, be it understood), was so shocking and so shameful, that as an Englishman I blush to remember it" (120).

In the essay "City of London Churches," the Uncommercial Traveller recollects how as a child, he had to visit the church on Sundays and bear the excruciating experience of having to listen to the preacher in a stuffy and crowded hall. The autobiographical recollections of the Uncommercial Traveller have strong affinities with Rousseau's *Reveries* (Thesis, ch. 1) in which Rousseau practises walking to recollect and sort out the painful experiences of his past. If not, how can he travel back to his childhood if he is not travelling on the timescale? Travelling/walking is, in fact, a trigger to raise the dust of memories settled long ago in mind. With his reveries about his childhood, the Uncommercial Traveller – who now seems to have merged with the writer – begins this leg of his journey to the churches of London. He visits various churches and describes the sorry state of their buildings and furniture. The allegory is too obvious to miss that "Christianity" was missing from them. He also questions the practice of forcing children to visit churches (instead of letting them play) to attend long preaching sessions, which they neither understand nor do they need to understand. It is easy to see that the Uncommercial Traveller is not only writing about his childhood memories but also writing from the perspective of a child. The expressions like "the invisible stuff," "five little stone lozenges" and "sniggering boys" prove that they are being described through the eyes of a child. Every sight gives rise to an associated memory in the narrator's mind. The narrator recollects the memory "of his own village church…" (128). The sight of a young couple reminded the narrator of the time when he was eighteen (129). Thus, it can be argued that while walking on the land and walking in the mind happens side by side, especially in this essay which cannot be termed as autobiographical because it is not written by an adult about himself. I think we lack a term to describe a nostalgic account of childhood by the same "child" in his say fifties. Drew has missed this subtle nuance when he states that "it seems possible that, writing in 1860, Dickens is recalling particular experiences of church-visiting in

1847-48 and combining them with both earlier and maturer memories" (295).

Dickens talks about his obsession with walking and the power of walking to unleash his creative potential in the essay "Shy Neighbourhoods." In this essay, he addresses the reader directly and talks about his habit of unconscious walking sometimes at night (Hollington 71). To quote, "My walking is of two kinds: one, straight on end to a definite goal at a round pace; the other, objectless, loitering, and purely vagabond. In the latter state, no gipsy on earth is a greater vagabond than myself; it is so natural to me and strong with me that I think I must be the descendant, at no great distance, of some irreclaimable tramp" (138). Thus, Dickens seems to agree with Nicholson that walking is an unconscious activity (11). But he makes a very pertinent remark that when he walks unconsciously, i.e. when he sleepwalks or when he walks without any predestination in his mind, he only walks and thinks, he can recollect a language of the deep mind which he forgets as soon be becomes conscious again. In all probability, Dickens suggests that it is the language of images, which is the language of the "real" in Lacan's terms, which is beyond the reach of the symbolic. It can thus be argued that Dickens has mastered the art of walking consciously as well as unconsciously. He walks consciously when he visits a place to see and report about it; he walks unconsciously when he "loiters" like a tramp without any destination to reach but to explore the mind. Dickens mentions in "Tramps" that he thinks himself to be a descendent of some tribe of tramps; he notes his experiences/conversations with the tramps he met during his walks. The tramps seem to be the lost descendants of a walker who walked as pilgrims ("Walking," Thoreau). Both Butor and Benjamin "approve the genetic derivation of the city flâneur from the gipsy on the heath" (Qtd. in Drew 307).

The essay "Dullborough Town" depicts the Uncommercial Traveller's visit Dullborough Town, the place where he spent his childhood. The narrator looks forward to recalling the "tender" memories of his childhood. The narrator is able to recall certain memories by casting a look at the place to which they are related. He decides to walk into the town. The narrator shares his dismay at the old buildings, in which he played as a child, being knocked down to make place for new buildings. Thus, the place where he ran wild as a child has been destroyed, and as a result, the narrator feels that the establishment has "committed an act of boyslaughter, in running over [his] childhood in this rough manner..." (173). He found the town had "shrunk fearfully" (176). For Dickens, memory is attached to the place as well as it is a cognitive function of the mind, it remains there as long as the place where it was created remains. Forrest Clingerman observers that the "...place and memory are written on each other, and are tied together by the complexity of our bodily experience of both" (121). The construction company, rues the narrator, has no right to alter the place and thus destroy the memories of his childhood. Dickens' narrator walks through the town, looks at various places and nostalgically recalls his childhood association with them. Such rumination is only possible when a person is walking; a traveller cruising through a place in a car at high speed cannot think like a walker. Dickens seems well aware of "the fundamental kinship between travel and reading/writing" (166).

In "Nights Walks," Dickens' narrator talks about his insomnia and his compulsive night walking for several nights. Initially, Dickens regards "Houselessness" as a state of being out of the house in the physical sense. Then he personifies "Houselessness" that can observe and even "walk." He even speaks of the "houseless mind" (188). Thus, there is little doubt that Dickens is employing "Houselessness" as a trope that has strong reverberations which King Lear's experience with the wandering wretches in the stormy night after being cast out by his cruel daughters (Act 3, Sc. 4, L. 32). In other words, it is the experience of being shaken out of a normal sense of self and experiencing the world unlike one has ever experienced before. Houselessness is more of a metaphor than a reference to the social problem of homelessness in London, as argued by John Drew (313). Houselessness can also be interpreted as an inability to sit within the house or a strong desire to be in the street. At another level, Houselessness is the all-pervasive Night/Darkness that holds everybody in its fold. It can also be compared with Shakespeare's personification of "Murder" as a Wolf walking to murder Duncan in *Macbeth* (Act 2, Sc.1. Line 42). With this shifting point of view, one finds the narrator speaking from the collective perspective of "us houseless people" (187) with whom Dickens shares his obsession for the streets. Dickens' narrator describes various places in their sights/shadows, sounds and smells as his "houseless mind" registered them while walking through the night: "[t]here are no streets or crowds of people here, to divert the attention. My head suffers, and that is very unusual, as you know with me" (Qtd. in Hollington 71).

Dickens praises Shakespeare for apostrophising sleep as "the death of each day's life." Then Dickens wonders why he should not call "Dreams the insanity of each day's sanity" (194). Having strong affinities with Lady Macbeth's sleepwalking, "Night Walks" by Dickens can be argued to be a dream that he dreamed with open eyes. At the end of the essay, Dickens comes home at sunrise tired, exhausted, and is at last able to sleep.

The essay "The Arcadian London" invites comparison with Henry David Thoreau's *Walden* (ch.2). The Uncommercial Traveller takes a peaceful and solitary retreat in Bond Street in London. From his lodging, he makes walking trips to the surrounding places. The narrator enjoys a "sense of freedom" (236) during his walking tours and feels rejuvenated again. He feels the emergence of "the original savage" (236) in him again as if he has been able to travel back on the time scale to that spot in human race memory when human beings were sojourners in the wild (ch. 2). Like Thoreau, the Uncommercial Traveller says, "I shut myself into this place of seclusion, after breakfast, and meditate" (237).

The Italian Rising for unification reminds the narrator of his own wanderings in Italy, which are the subject matter of the essay. The prisoner of the title of the essay "The Italian Prisoner" is described as a political offender during the Italian Rising for unification in the 1840s. The essay brings out the sincere efforts by an Englishman to have the Italian prisoner, who was awaiting execution, pardoned and freed. Dickens employs this story of English generosity for a foreign prisoner to discuss the Italian struggle for unification and lend his tacit support for the same.

The seventeen essays of *The Uncommercial Traveller* display the sincerest and novel endeavour to forge a genre that is realistic yet creative, prosaic yet not without poetic flashes, satirical yet solemn, firmly rooted in journalistic practices yet decorated with all the literary resources under the arm of a seasoned writer like Charles Dickens. That the art of walking and thinking plays an indispensable role to root the writer as well as his writings into the time and the place and that the genius of Dickens style lends the uncommercial essays a universal appeal is too obvious to state. Only a literary giant like Charles Dickens can reach such a height while walking on the ground.

CHAPTER 4

The Birth of Artistic Flâneur: Baudelaire's *The Painter of Modern Life*

Baudelaire writes with a painter's brush. He captures impressions and sketches them through the medium of words. His works like *The Flowers of Evil* (1993) can be better understood in relation to painting, especially that of Constantin Guys on whom Baudelaire has modelled the notion of flâneur in the essay *The Painter of Modern Life* (1863). Though flâneur registered his presence – as a leisurely walker in the city of Paris – in the French culture quite early, the notion of "artist flâneur" (Castigliano ch. 4) was first imagined in Baudelaire's *The Painter of Modern Life* in 1863. Those who presume that a few classical geniuses who portray "*general* beauty," observes Baudelaire, embody "the whole secret" (Baudelaire 1) of the history of literature commit a grave critical error (emphasis original). To correct it, one should accord an equally prominent place to the artists depicting the immediate and the "present beauty." Baudelaire further notes that progress towards remedying the error has already begun. As a result, previously lesser-known but talented artists are keenly studied.

This period of transition, the according to Baudelaire, is ideal for introducing "a rational and historical theory of beauty" against "the academic theory of an (sic) unique and absolute beauty," (3). Aesthetic beauty, according to Baudelaire, consists of two elements: "the *general* beauty" which is expressed by the classical poets, and "the particular beauty, the beauty of circumstance and the sketch of manners" (1). According to Baudelaire, the depiction of beauty in the present is as important as the representation of beauty in its eternal and universal aspect. It is the fleeting manifestation of beauty in the present what Baudelaire calls "modernity." Every artist has his/her own idea of modernity because the eternal aspect of beauty remains constant for all artists across the ages. We define modern as "relating to the present or recent times as opposed to the remote past."[49] However, Baudelaire's modernity seems more akin to the future. By modern, Baudelaire suggests the quality of being "ahead of one's times." The eye of the flâneur is trained to catch the flashes of modernity in a crowd. For example, someone's dress may display, through subtle touches, its quality to appear ahead of the contemporary style of fashion; someone, by virtue of his/her thinking and writing, may sound out of tune with the contemporary ideology, yet their ideas may prove path-breaking in the times to come. The flâneur would be swift to notice and depict it in the works of art. Modernity, thus, might peep through a subtle gesture, through an instance of mannerism or a cut or crease in someone's dress might cause ripples in the mind of the flâneur. In other words, when an artistic flâneur witnesses "future" walking across the "present," he wastes no time in capturing and painting it on the canvass. An artistic flâneur thus strives to offer a glimpse of the eternal to the reader/spectator through the "sketch of manners" at a particular time. Such an artist is a "man of the crowd" and loves travelling and blending with the crowd incognito. S/he can be an

> observer, philosopher, flâneur – call him what you will; but whatever words you use in trying to define his kind of artist, you will certainly be led to bestow upon him some adjective which you could not apply to the painter of eternal, or at least more lasting things, of heroic or religious subjects. Sometimes he is a poet; more often he comes closer to the novelist or the moralist; he is the painter of the passing moment and of all the suggestions of eternity that it contains. (Baudelaire 4)

Flâneur thus is a descriptive term applied to artists, painters, poets, novelists and moralists belonging to diverse cultures and predilections, yet they are kindred spirits and have a similar approach towards their craft. Though there are instances of flâneurs delineating "poverty and humble life" too (5), yet the world that a flâneur lives in and portrays in the works of art is the bourgeoisie fashionable world of the modern city (Castigliano, ch. 4).

In the essay *The Painter of Modern Life* (1863), Baudelaire selects an artist, namely Constantin Guys, whom he regards "perfect flâneur" (9) and analyses his works in terms of the peculiarities of his art. However, at the same time, Baudelaire, due to Constantin Guys' request for anonymity, decides to treat him as a "pure poetic

49 See: *Oxford Dictionary of English*, Third Edition, 2010.

hypothesis, conjecture, a labour of the imagination" in the essay (6). With one stroke, the individual Constantin Guys becomes a metaphorical artistic flâneur in the essay. Baudelaire, however, does mention his name in his essay. What kind of anonymity is it? Baudelaire granted Constantin Guys anonymity of a different kind by describing a "type," an imaginary character with inputs from Guys' life and, also from other flâneurs including Baudelaire's own experience as a flâneur – Baudelaire wrote *The Flowers of Evil* as a practising flâneur. To put it differently, Baudelaire is making use of the skeleton of Constantin Guys' life to creatively flesh out the theory of the artistic flâneur and, also, to reimagine the theory of beauty based on the study of many such flâneur artists, novelist, painters, moralists and poets. Thus, whatever Baudelaire writes about Constantin Guys is true for any artist whose methodology is similar to that of Constantin Guys. The group includes Benjamin, Baudelaire and many others. Remarkably, *The Flowers of Evil* and *Paris Spleen* are the works by Baudelaire as an artistic flâneur. The poems are a creative record of what strikes "the ambulatory gaze" (Anne Friedberg) that the flâneur (Baudelaire) casts on the contemporary Parisian cityscape. The narratorial voice in the sketch-like poems walks from thought to thought, scene to scene, from sketch to sketch. The narrator even steps into the shoes of the characters and sketches them through the medium of poetic language.

Constantin Guys, "the perfect flâneur" (Baudelaire 9), possesses many eccentricities. He is so shy of fame that he does not even sign his paintings, which are so striking in craft and execution that they are immediately identified. Monsieur G. is an old man who has discovered his hidden talents at a later age. In his forties, Monsieur G. became restless with a flood of images rushing through his mind. He had to give them an outlet to keep his sanity. Baudelaire notes that while depicting them on the canvass, Monsieur G. would gesture savagely, work wildly with the paint and brush as if he was amid a raging battle. Sometimes, he would behave like a child who is annoyed at not being able to manoeuvre his fingers as he wishes (6). At this sentence, the editor of the essay puts a footnote: "Baudelaire must be mistaken here" (6) because, the editor asserts, Guys at that time was already an accomplished painter so cannot work clumsily. The editor commits the error of considering Monsieur G., who is supposedly being described in the essay, as a particular individual. On the contrary, Baudelaire is writing about a "type," not an "individual" Monsieur G.

Baudelaire further states that, unlike an ordinary artist who is limited to his area of interest, Monsieur G. feels at home everywhere. He is an avid walker and a "cosmopolitan" (Baudelaire 6) who has left his home to make everywhere his home. Since he is a "man of the entire world" and "spiritual citizen" of the universe (7), he wants to know, understand and appreciate everything that happens not only in the world but also in the universe. Originality is the hallmark of his art. The force behind his creativity is curiosity. He is passionately drawn towards the crowd, and he connects with it spiritually. He possesses the ability to become a "child" who experiences everything with a child-like wonder. Yet he has the power of self-expression of an artist. As a result, he can, through his art, transmit that sense of amazement that he experiences to others. He is so ravished by the beauty in the city that he dedicates his life to study it. He finds the contours of buildings, collage of faces in the crowd, spectacle of fashion as myriad manifestations of beauty. He empties himself of identity to drink on beauty ceaselessly. When he sits at his table for expressing artistically what he has gulped down in his walks during the day, the art so created becomes tempered with the signatures of his soul. Baudelaire states that Monsieur G does not sign his works "as they are bedazzled by his soul" (5).

By virtue of his extraordinary abilities, he can put to order an inordinate mass of mental stuff accumulated since childhood. He casts his "ecstatic gaze" (Baudelaire 8) on the objects and people around him and notices even minute details missed by an ordinary eye. The flâneur's walking movement leads to an enhanced sensual receptivity in the mind, which transforms the abstract phenomena into felt experiences. Benjamin notes in *The Arcades Project*, "…[t]hat ananmestic (sic) intoxication in which the flâneur goes about the city not only feeds on the sensory data taking shape before his eyes but often possesses itself of abstract knowledge – indeed, of dead facts – as something experienced and lived through" (417). Baudelaire observes a flâneur masters the ability to attain child-like wonder at will so that we can term him "man-child," (8). His genius thus lies in the ability to recover childhood at will, so he has the ability to erase at will all the cognitive conditioning received since childhood to rediscover the ecstatic plenitude that a child lives in. Thus, it is Benjamin, not Baudelaire, who considers walking movement as the catalyst for a flâneur to develop heightened sensibilities to view his world. One can argue that the flâneur remains in that state for so long as he is on his feet. When he stops walking, he relapses to his previous state of mind, but he can always recollect the felt-impressions when he was in an excited state of mind. Baudelaire observes that a flâneur as a "child" is "always drunk" and finds the world always in a "state of newness" (8).

The flaneur has an acute sensitivity towards things sublime. In him, this hypersensitivity manifests itself as a kind of "nervous shock" at the sight of something sublime; the shock is conveyed to the "core of the brain" where by degrees it is illumined into a "diadem of dazzling clarity" (*The Flowers of Evil*, "Benediction," Baudelaire 15) which finally leads to an artistic expression. Thus, the flâneur has the task cut out for him: to extract "poetry from history" and to sift "eternal from the transitory" (12). Without the artistic ability to distil and express this "transitory, fugitive element" in the "present" the beauty of the eternal is indeterminable (13). Baudelaire wanted to describe Monsieur Guys as "an artist pure and simple," but Baudelaire found him to be more than that. He cannot be termed as a "dandy" because a dandy possesses a strong sense of character and a deep understanding of the moral principles of the entire world. But a flaneur, on the other hand, is given to experiencing life passionately. Since it is hard to describe him by existing terms, Baudelaire finally decides to describe him as "a pure pictorial moralist" (9).

The experience of "shock" is significant for understanding Baudelaire's artistic work (*Illuminations*, "Some Motifs in Baudelaire," Benjamin 163). The shock that the flâneur receives from the crowd feels as if one is exposed to a reservoir of electric energy. A shock can be described as the passage of more current through the network of nerves than it can endure. A shock throws the working of the "circuit of nerves" out of balance for some time. How much time does the "circuit of nerves" takes to recover depends on the intensity of the shock and its preparedness to bear such shocks because of its like experiences in the past. The person endowed with such sensibilities, observes Baudelaire, is like a "kaleidoscope equipped with consciousness" (175). As a result, the electric energy that benumbs the crowd charges the flâneur. So much so that sometimes the flâneur acts wildly with the artistic tools at the table as if a battle is being fought. Constantin Guys, notes Baudelaire, stabs, jolts and gestures savagely; spurts ink on the paper and even splashes colours on the roof and the walls of his room while striving to catch up with the rush of images before his mind's eye lest he should miss even one of them. It can be understood through an analogy: a flâneur is an overdeveloped circuit of nerves in terms of more developed consciousness; he needs "charge" to activate the circuit that he gets from the crowd. In the crowd, it is lying unused because they do not have the circuit to run it. Thus, the phrase "crowd is flâneur's element" can be rewritten as that flâneur is the "element" (in the sense of a "circuit"), and that crowd gives him the "power" to activate it. Thus, the flâneur is conscious even of those experiences of the people that are lying unconscious in the collective unconscious. Thus, any artist, novelist, poet, painter, philosopher, moralist who possesses such awareness and makes use of it in his art is an artistic flâneur.

The traumatized personalities are excluded from Baudelaire's idea of artistic flâneur because they tend to re-enact their own traumas rather than watching the drama of life disinterestedly. In other words, they project their irreconcilable complexes onto their world and view objects and people around them not as *they are* (emphasis added) but as they wish/fear them to be. To quote Linda Belau, a "… traumatic experience is grounded in the repetition of an impossibility." Note what Constantin Guys has to say about such persons: "any man who is not crushed by one of those griefs whose nature is too real not to monopolize all his capacities, and who can yet be *bored in the heart of the multitude* (emphasis original), is a blockhead! a blockhead! and I despise him!" (Guys qtd. in "Painter," Baudelaire 10). Thus, a traumatized subject is excused for not being impressed by spectacle of the modern world.

Baudelaire thus borrows the name, location, and biography from a practising flâneur, namely Constantin Guys, because he does not want to sound theoretical in discussing the felt-experience of an artistic flâneur. Under his name, he pools the peculiarities of flâneurs whom he knew (including himself). The cultural figure of flâneur as a city saunterer already existed in France before Baudelaire. Baudelaire drew on this tradition to fashion his notion of artistic flâneur. Federico Castigliano traces the roots of the words flâneur. He notes that the term flâneur might have been related to the Norman verb "flanner" ("to laze"), first recorded in 1638. The term flâneur also shares links with the ancient Scandinavian "flana" ("to run here and there"). Castigliano quotes from The Grand Dictionnaire universel du XIX siècle, by Pierre Larousse, that the term flâneur has been derived from the Irish adjective "flanni," meaning "libertine" (*Flâneur*, ch. 4). The first example of the word flâneur the modern French dates from the early nineteenth century. It can be argued that the term flâneur gained ground in Paris from 1930s onwards. Also, at this time the practice of walking in the city arcades and boulevards as a form of fashionable pastime was becoming popular. The word flâneur appeared in French art and literature around the middle of the nineteenth century. A masculine noun in French, flâneur suggests a saunterer in the city of Paris. A flâneur walks in the city to capture and paint transient beauty in his works of art. What constitutes reality for others is a symbolic ensemble for the flâneur. The city for a flâneur is a text that calls for creative expression in the form of art. He practises walking in the city to unlock his creativity. Moreover, the city, which was designed for quick movement between point A and point B, now allowed pointless wandering. Travelling in a vehicle can now be discounted for a ramble on foot. All these small acts pose a challenge to the founding logic of the modern city, i.e. swift destination-bound movement. Due to such a paradoxical position, the flâneur attracted the interest of thinkers and philosophers of modernity (Castigliano, ch. 4). More than three decades later, Baudelaire in his collection of essays *The Painter of Modern Life* (1863), unfolded the creative potential of the flâneur as an artist tool to capture and express aesthetic experiences in works of art.

Sometimes suggesting verbal equivalents of certain concepts in one's language and culture helps to better understand the terms like flânerie, which is the verb, derived from the noun flâneur. For instance, if Thoreau's walking ("Walking") is an *udaasi*,[50] in Punjabi language, i.e. melancholic wandering preoccupied with inner predicaments; Baudelaire's flânerie can be translated as *awaaragi*,[51] in

---

50 Henry David Thoreau propounds and practises walking in "Walking and *Walden, or Life in the Woods* (1854)

See. Joshi, S.S. *Punjabi - English Dictionary*. Publication Bureau Punjabi University, Patiala. 1999. pp. 9

51 This ghazal articulates quintessential qualities of flânerie, i.e. lonesomeness, existential vacuity, rootlessness, and an urge to escape into the crowd incognito (*be-shakl*) to forget the problematics of the self.

See. "Awaragi." Written by Mohsin Naqvi, Sung by Ghulam Ali, *Bollywoodtarjuma*, July29, 2016. https://bollywoodtarjuma.wordpress.com/2016/07/29/awaragi-mohsin-naqvighulam-ali/

the Urdu language, i.e. dawdling and deriving pleasure from the spectacle of the city.

Walter Benjamin took the idea of flâneur from Baudelaire's collection of poems *The Flowers of Evil* and recast him in the role of "a detective of the street life" (Shields 61). In *The Arcades Project*, not only does Benjamin write about flâneur and write it as a flâneur (Seal) but also his way of researching and collecting the material, i.e. observing the contemporary life and taking down notes, is like a flâneur. So in *The Arcades Project,* a practising flâneur was writing to theorize his craft. In *The Arcades Project*, while dwelling on the psychological effect that the overwhelming sensory stimuli have on its citizens, Benjamin enunciates two concepts: *Erlebnis* and *Erfahrung.* The former refers to the sensory numbness produced by the shock caused by the quick succession of sights, sounds and smells; the latter refers to the moments when the shock was effectively countered by the defence mechanism of the mind ("Some Motifs," Benjamin 163).

Erlebnis thus means those experiences that failed to enter into consciousness due to the excessive shock. And *Erfahrung* refers to that experiences which the consciousness was able to register and, therefore, they can be regarded as lived moments (163). Benjamin notes that due to the failure to feel the experiences, the masses in the modern city are condemned to confusion and alienation. The faster the kaleidoscope of images and sounds flows into the consciousness, and the more alert the consciousness has to be to register it, the lesser do they enter into the experience and memory (*Illuminations*, "Some Motifs on Baudelaire," Benjamin 163).

Therefore, the slowing down of movement, the leisurely lingering over the scenes and places that assumes more importance. The slowing down of the movement is a challenge to the fast-moving life of a city, and with the slowed-down movement, the eye can see the contradictions and find out the hidden connections/fissures between apparent diversity/unity offered by a modern city. The flâneur can spend as much time over an instance of sight or scene as he wishes and thereby forms experience and later on express that experience in art. A flâneur imagines the modern scene in a subversive way because he gives a free run to his imagination to savour the dream-like reality which Benjamin terms "phantasmagoria" (*The Arcades Project*, Benjamin). By walking in a fast-moving city, a flâneur interprets modernity. Though born and fashioned out of the modern city, a flâneur challenges the founding logic of it. He walks against the tempo of life dictated by the modern city. He is attracted to modernity and his attraction is not submissive but defiant. The slowing down of movement to the pace of walking is opposite to the founding logic of modernity that eulogises speed. Therefore, a flâneur walks doubly, walks into the modernity and away from it spatially as well as temporally. To quote, "[t]he flâneur's movement creates anachrony: he travels urban space, the space of modernity, but is forever looking to the past" (Seale). In other words, he is detached despite being in the thick of modern city life, and therefore, can look beneath "the construct" called modernity (Bacal). Benjamin observes a flâneur is always "out of place" (*Illuminations*, "Some Motifs in Baudelaire," Benjamin 172).

Commenting on the indifferent nature of the crowd in London, Engels notes that to survive, the masses have to part with their soul, i.e. they have embraced dehumanisation (qtd. in "Motifs on Baudelaire," Benjamin 166). Yet they long for contact with a soulful person to be alive again. The function of a flâneur is to light the crowd with the flame of his soul (Benjamin 195n1). The flâneur with a comprehensive soul enters the crowd, awakens it, and, through his art, articulates its repressed emotions. To quote Castigliano, "It is precisely this ability to annul oneself, to come out from the stifling prison of the inner life, this is the science and the skill of the flâneur." Benjamin too agrees when he says that "Not finding the road that you are looking for does not mean much. But to lose one's way in the city, as one loses one's way in a forest, requires some schooling." (qtd. in Castigliano). In other words, a flâneur is he who dedicates his life to catch the shooting stars of fleeting beauty, to freeze the moment in his soul and distil the artistic beauty out of it. Thus, a flâneur is the reverse of a Thoreau's walker (ch. 2), insofar as a walker is after universal and eternal things, a flâneur is after that the fleeting moments of beauty, which Baudelaire terms as modernity. A flâneur succeeds in claiming the present beauty from the flow of eternity where he is able to capture the moment first in his consciousness, then express it as art.

Since a flâneur cannot reject the modern city like a walking recluse, he chooses to live amid the crowd and practise detachment from it (Castigliano). The essential difference between a flâneur and a spiritual walker is that the flâneur walks into the crowd to escape the empty self, whereas a spiritual walker that Thoreau speaks of ("Walking," Thoreau) walks away from society into the forest to connect with his self. Human beings can understand their inner self through two ways: direct introspection or through projecting their unconscious self to external nature, and, then examine and assimilate it into their personality. Direct introspection is the art of an accomplished traveller who can travel without moving physically from one place to another because after having travelled a lot, he has internalised those places which now he can re-travel in the mind. Michel Butor observes that "… in order to travel better, I actually travel less" ("Travel and Writing," 2). While the success or otherwise of projection depends on the clarity of the "mirror;" the clearer the "mirror," the brighter the image, and more rewarding/disrupting the projection. There is not a third way to access the self. The journey of a spiritual walker is from the "self" towards the "world" outside whereas the progress of a flâneur is from "world" to the "self." A flâneur stares at existential emptiness, while a spiritual walker is in possession of his spiritual predilections, and to preserve them, he practises solitary walking. Both a spiritual walker and a flâneur walk in the quest for something. Whereas a solitary walker can project the self onto the benign natural surroundings to examine and recollect it, but a flâneur has to grapple with the "phantasmagoria" of the modern city, which is highly amorphous and distorted like a dream. In other words, his infatuation with the modern city, and his refusal to abandon it for the forest like a hermit, necessitates a living fraught with the problematic interface between the self and the external reality. Benjamin observes that the fast succession of images in cityscape produces a sensual numbness. The impossible task of a flâneur is to wake from numbness, see the truth behind the image, and through it gain more knowledge about the self. His self is not his self but the larger self of the crowd, i.e. the collective unconscious of the modern city, which can be regarded as the heart of modernity. Unlike a solitary walker, a flâneur is pitted against a heavily distorted reality, the "phantasmagoria" of the modern city, with only projection as a tool to grapple with it. In this way, he does not escape from his existential imperatives but faces them single-handedly. The flâneur has to conquer the overwhelming life of the modern city to survive as an artist. Benjamin notes in *The Arcades Project* that a flâneur goes to the marketplace to hunt for "the physiologies" (372). Rousseau's walker and the flâneur are alike insofar as they both walk to have a close look at their world, the former "botanizes" in nature, the latter on the asphalt (372).

In the age that saw the fragmentation of experience in all walks of life, the search for God lies in the search for wholeness. The artistic flâneur in his search for wholeness collects, combines, presents the images from the modern city and offers his comments on them (*Illuminations*, "Some Motifs in Baudelaire," Benjamin 4). The crowd is the element of the flâneur. Like Thoreau ("Walking"), Baudelaire addresses his work to "kindred spirits" (155). Like Thoreau, Benjamin too believes that the true end of philosophy is to express the "true" experience of human beings, not the "denatured" experience of civilised masses (156). The flâneur, with his deep insight into the modern city, can unleash the latent "utopian potential" (Lauster 140) which can lead to "revolutionary transformation" (Benjamin 141). Susan Buck-Morss notes Benjamin believed that the fragments he collected in *The Arcades Project* were politically loaded and "… capable of transmitting revolutionary energy across generations" (99). Baudelaire wrote his poems as a flâneur.

There is another lesser-known precursor of flânerie; he is Søren Kierkegaard. He walked in the city of Copenhagen. Kierkegaard's "aimless drift that was to become that hallmark of the flâneur on the streets of Paris a generation later" (29) writes Merlin Coverley. Rebecca Solnit also observes that, were [… Kierkegaard] less prolific and less Danish, might be the best candidate" for having pioneered the art of flânerie before Charles Baudelaire. It was not about practising flânerie because "everyone engaged in some version of flâneury (sic)" (Solnit). It was practising as well as theorising about flânerie that made Baudelaire and Benjamin the two practising thinkers. A flâneuse is the female counterpart of a flâneur. Writing against the masculine monopoly of the cultural practice of flânerie,[52] Lauren Elkin retraces the footsteps of flâneuse. Walking through literary and cultural history, biography, literary criticism, she contests male dominance on the streets of history. Elkin excavates culturally and ideologically male-dominated historical sites and reconstructs them to establish that the flâneuse was as much a presence on the streets as the flâneur.

---

52 Flânerie is a gender-neutral noun, which designates the practice of wandering in city on feet by both the sexes.

See, *Oxford Dictionary of English*, Third Edition, 2010.

Thus, one can see that flâneur was a walker on the streets of Paris. Baudelaire drew on the French popular culture to endow the flâneur with literary and philosophical overtones. One can say that Baudelaire fashioned the artistic flâneur from a cultural type who was a stroller on the streets of Paris. After Baudelaire, Benjamin practised and theorized the artistic flâneur extensively, especially in *The Arcades Project*. Thus, I have combined the insights of both the practitioners for developing an understanding about flâneur and his metamorphosis into artistic flâneur.

Conclusion

While writing down the concluding part of the present volume, I was beset by the thought that there cannot be a conclusion, rather a summation and clarification of various arguments which may be presented to the reader in hindsight. No two persons walk alike, just as no two persons think alike. The nuanced peculiarities in the gait of an individual create a signature style of walking. Therefore, as we have seen in the course of this study, walking and thinking have myriad manifestations in individual practitioners. It is impossible to pin down such a diversely applied practice to the reductive confines of a definition. If compelled to manufacture a definition, despite being sternly warned against by Henry David Thoreau, I would say that walking as a metaphysical act lies beyond the range of linguistic definition; walking as a physiological act has already been defined in the "Introduction"[53] section of the study; and, finally, walking in the context of the time and the place vis-à-vis the walker would have as many definitions as there are instances of contextualised embodied experience created and recorded by the walkers.

The title *Thinking While Walking: Gathering Embodied Experience for Writing* sounds somewhat abstract. But, after having seen the arguments offered in the previous pages, it can be asserted that the actions, walking, and thinking while walking, being performative in nature, presuppose the existence of not only a living human body but also robust enough to undertake long walks, and intelligent enough to think and generate ideas around an aesthetic problem, and, creative enough to embody the experience so developed in some literary form. This has been the primary assumption on which the present volume is based. The literature of walking or the "pedestrian cannon" (Coverley 14) as it is being called is thus the corpus of writings by able-bodied men and women having excellent abilities of the head and heart – their list is surprisingly long, spanning the history of literature till the present times.

---

53 See, Introduction for a detailed discussion on the evolutionary journey of walking and its relation with thinking.

Moreover, the practice of walking has been traced back to its evolutionary roots, which led to significant findings. The ability to bipedal walking that came earlier than the development of larger human brain was primarily responsible for the development of the human brain, especially the cerebral cortex, the most recently developed and the uppermost layer of the brain, which not only controls the sensory and motor functions such vision, hearing etc., but also performs the cognitive functions such as thinking, analysing, and reasoning vis-à-vis the previous like experiences stored in the memory. In short, bipedal walking is not only the evolutionary force behind the development of human beings as thinking subjects but also organically connected with the thinking function, so much so that walking and thinking become mutually enabling processes.

The action of walking not only aligns the body of the walker with the mind but also connects him/her with the place so that the experience so created is subjective to the person yet situated in the place. This composite quality of walking has been tapped by thinkers, writers and philosophers through the ages. While walking and thinking is as old as (or even older than) the Greek Peripatetics,[54] the notion of *thinking* about walking as an enabling activity is of recent origin (emphasis added). The aim of the present volume has been to interpret the practice of walking and thinking as reflected in the works of certain practitioners of walking, thinking and writing, for developing a felt understanding of this emerging practice. However, my feet walked quite a few miles around the reserve forests of F. R. I., Dehradun, Uttarakhand while I was thinking about the project in the initial stages.

That walking, the performative action on the land, can shape and structure a work of literature as a literary motif as well was first demonstrated by J. J. Rousseau. Walking inspired works are hybrid and discursive in form and content. For Rousseau, walking, apart from being a physical practice and a literary trope in his *Reveries*, was a sacred pilgrimage to the temple of his "self." Self, in Rousseau, becomes a medium for interaction between the text and the world, and this interaction, rather than being passive, becomes engaging to the point of being redemptive in terms of relieving the self of the deep-rooted dilemmas which were interrupting self-peace. By the last

54 See, Introduction for a detailed discussion on walking and thinking in Greek culture.

walk, we find Rousseau mellow and at peace with himself after having reconciled to the long-standing traumas during his walking, thinking and writing stint. What Rousseau probably did under the overwhelming inner pressure becomes a creative tool in the hands of his successors. Moreover, in the field of literature and medicine, certain works are prescribed for reading to help heal post-hospitalization trauma – Rousseau demonstrates the healing power of literature in *Reveries*.

H. D. Thoreau wants us to live and walk in nature much like the pre-civilised human being. More than ever, modern human beings need to rediscover the wild buried in their nature because, according to Thoreau, a tamed social life lived for so long has impoverished us spiritually as well as physically. To connect to our wild roots, to nourish our sagging spirits, and to know our original selves, we need the touch of the wild. Thoreau holds the social conditions responsible for making us docile to the point of being lifeless. He demonstrates that we can escape economic and social slavery, at least for some time in our life, to live a life pure and simple. Writing, for Thoreau, is only for keeping a record of his experiences meant for anyone wishing to follow his footsteps into the forest. In being so radical and uncompromising in his approach, Thoreau stands tall amongst all other writing walkers studied in this project. Thoreau thus reconciles the two extremes in saying that we should be wild while staying fully civilized. In other words, we should develop the raw strength of the wild without losing the fruits of civilization. Thus, some literary works can spiritually re-orientate and guide us if there is an interpreter to explain their true significance – the walker in the literature of walking is the prototype of such an interpreter.

The artistic flâneur, as imagined by the two celebrated practitioners: Charles Baudelaire and Walter Benjamin, is an interpreter of the modern city. The benumbing speed of the modern city stops the senses from experiencing a moment and form memory, which creates an alienating effect. The flâneur walks against the modern city to experience it sensuously before reaching an understanding of its diverse phenomena and its effects on the city dweller. The essential difference between a flâneur and a spiritual walker is that the flâneur walks into the crowd of the modern city, whereas a spiritual walker walks away from the modern city into the forest. The former walks to fill the empty self; the latter walks to empty the self of social conditioning. Whereas the spiritual walker has the benevolent nature on which he can mirror his dilemmas to examine and resolve them, but the task of an artistic flâneur is far challenging because he has the shape-shifting "phantasmagoria" of the modern city in which he has first to find the truth in which to reflect his self-image. In other words, his infatuation with the modern city, and his refusal to abandon it for the forest like a hermit, necessitates a living fraught with the problematics of the interface between the self and the city. Thus, flâneur in the modern city remains the last descendent of the original walker in the wild – s/he has to walk to avoid being extinct.

Dickens' walking persona, popularly called *badaud*, the incognito walker ready to jump into the shoes of anyone on the way, was a development parallel to the practice of flâneur in Paris. Like flâneur, *badaud* practises thinking while walking in the city to contemplate his "self" in the living context of his society and times. Parallel to his walking practice, Dickens fashions a style, which is journalistic yet literary, detached yet personal, anecdotal yet unprejudiced for conveying something more than mere newspaper reporting, with a sense of immediacy and urgency unknown to a literary text. And like Thoreau, Dickens sets his entire project against the dehumanising effects of consumerism on the Victorian society of his times. Dickens project is to assimilate various genres to forge new form and style of writing yet keep it nebulous to negotiate changes on the way.

Thus, we see, walking enables thinking, and, finally writing that eventually takes the form of a text. The self, the text and the world are the three co-ordinates of the universe the author creates in his work; walking is the catalyst that sets forth the traffic of mutual exchange between the three points of reference – even as the text is in the making. In fact, the crisscross walking movements weave the texture of the sentences on the pages of the text. Apart from these three points, there will be a fourth point of view as well. The fourth point of view will be conceived by the interpreter who may see the text from a point outside as well from inside the textual boundaries. The interpreter might shift his/her point of view to any of the four slots, even view it from multiple angles simultaneously. Initially the interpreter begins from author's point of view; but slowly constructs his/her own point of view, and it is significant in terms of how and where the interpreter chooses to place it; every new reader moves it as per his/her choice. Thus, the fourth point is always on the move. Thus, unlike a critic who views a work from preconceived critical perspectives lying outside the text, the role of an interpreter becomes very crucial in appreciating the literature of walking. The interpreter liberates the work from the hegemony of critical imperialism.

Select Bibliography

Primary Sources

Baudelaire, Charles. *The Painter of Modern Life and Other Essays*. Translated and Edited by Jonathan Mayne, Phaidon Press, 1964.

Dickens, Charles. *The Uncommercial Traveller*. Second Edition, Chapman and Hall, London, World Public Library, 2010.

Rousseau, Jean-Jacques. *Reveries of the Solitary Walker*. Penguin, 1979. Kindle edition, https://www.amazon.in/Reveries-Solitary-Walker-Penguin-Classics/dp/0140443630

Thoreau, Henry David. *Walden, or, Life in the Woods*. Edited by Robert F. Sayre, Cape Cod, 1985.

.... "Walking." Atlantic Monthly vol. 9, No. 56, 1862, pp. 657-674.

https://www.theatlantic.com/magazine/archive/1862/06/walking/304674/

Secondary Sources

Amato, Joseph. *On Foot: A History of Walking*. New York University Press, 2004. Print

Arendt, Hannah. *The Human Condition*. University of Chicago Press, 2013. *Google Scholar. https://books.google.com/books?hl=en&lr=&id=ARBJAgAAQBAJ&oi=fnd&pg=PR5&dq=Hannah+Arendt+in++++++++++her+book+Human+Condition,+1958,+Chicago+University+Press.&ots=dFguqIIuWA&sig=EJJ6h9HE8IKV1gUP6pkgwcMJxVM,* Accessed on 17-10-2021 at 12:20 pm.

Andrews, Malcolm. "Dickens and the Serial Flâneur." *The Dickensian*, vol. 114, no. 504, 2018, pp. 21-25. *ProQuest*, https://search.proquest.com/scholarly-journals/dickens-serial-flâneur/docview/2056427156/se-2?accountid=142596.

.... *Charles Dickens and His Performing Selves: Dickens and the Public Readings*, Oxford University Press, 2006.

Bacal, Michael. "Walter Benjamin, the Flâneur, and Redemption." *Telosscope*, November 29, 2011. http://www.telospress.com/walter-benjamin-the-flaneur-and- redemption/

Bachelard, Gaston. Introduction. *The Poetics of Space: The Classic Look at How We Experience Intimate Places*. Translated by Maria Jolas, Beacon Press, 1964, page 37.

Baudelaire, Charles. *The Flowers of Evil*. Translated by James McGowan, Oxford University Press, 1993.

.... *Paris Spleen*, trans. L. Varese, New Directions Books. 1970

Beckett, Samuel. *Waiting for Godot: Tragicomedy in Two Acts.* Grove Press, 1954.

Belau, Linda. "Trauma and the Material Signifier." *Postmodern Culture*, vol. 11 no. 2, 2001. *Project MUSE*, doi:10.1353/pmc.2001.0001

Benjamin, Walter. *The Arcades Project.* Translated by Howard Eiland and Kevin McLaughlin, Harvard University Press, 2002.

.... Illuminations: Essays and Reflections. Translated by Harry Zohn, Edited by Hannah Arendt, Harcourt, Brace & World, 1968.

Berenson, Frances. "Hegel on Others and the Self." *Philosophy*, vol. 57, no. 219, Jan. 1982, pp. 77-90. *JSTOR*.

Bipedalism vs. Brain Size. E-Fossils. Department of Liberal Anthropology, University of Texas, Austin. n.d., n.p. http://efossils.org/book/bipedalism-vs-brain-size. Accessed on 06-05-2019 at 2.23 pm.

Borror, Donald J. *Dictionary of Word Roots and Combining Forms.* First Edition, Mayfield, 1960. EBook.

Bradshaw, Leah. "Acting out the Intimate Self". "Review of Instinct and Intimacy: Political Philosophy and Autobiography in Rousseau, by Margaret Ogrodnick," *Review of Politics*, 2001, https://www.jstor.org/stable/1408397

Brain, C. K. "Raymond Dart and our African Origins". *A Century of Nature: Twenty-One Discoveries that Changed Science and the World.* Edited by Laura Garwin and Tim Lincoln, University of Chicago Press, 2003, https://www.press.uchicago.edu/Misc/Chicago/284158_brain.html.

Brann, Eva T. H. et al. Introduction, *Phaedo* by Plato, Focus Publications, 1998. Burt, E. S. "Mapping City Walks: The Topography of Memory in Rousseau's Second and Seventh Promenades," *Yale French Studies*, No. 74, *Phantom Proxies: Symbolism and the Rhetoric of History*, 1988, pp. 231-247, https://www.jstor.org/stable/2930297

Buck-Morss, Susan. *Dialectics of Seeing: Walter Benjamin and the Arcades Project.* The MIT Press, 1989.

.... "The Flâneur, the Sandwichman and the Whore: The Politics of Loitering," *New German Critique*, vol. no. 39, no. 2, pp. 99-140. *JSTOR*,

http://www.jstor.org/stable/488122, Accessed on 16-12-2014 at 7.20 pm.

Burt, E. S. "Mapping City Walks: The Topography of Memory in Rousseau's Second and Seventh Promenades," *Yale French Studies*, no. 74, *Phantom Proxies: Symbolism and the Rhetoric of History*, 1988, pp. 231-247, https://www.jstor.org/stable/2930297

Butor, Michel, et al. "Travel and Writing." *Mosaic: A Journal for the Interdisciplinary Study of Literature*, vol. 8, no. 1, 1974, pp. 1–16. *JSTOR*, www.jstor.org/stable/24777013. Accessed on 4 Apr. 2021at 10 a.m.

Caputo, John D. "Deconstructing Institutions: A Reply to Dauenhauer." Human Studies, Vol. 14, No. 4, 1991, pp. 331-337, Springer, URL:

http://www.jstor.org/stable/20010942. Accessed: 28/06/2014 11:16, JSTOR. Review.

Carrier, David. "Baudelaire's Philosophical Theory of Beauty." *Nineteenth-Century French Studies*, vol. 23, no. 3/4, 1995, pp. 382–402. *JSTOR*, www.jstor.org/stable/23537067.

Castigliano, Federico. *Flâneur: The Art of Wandering in the Modern City*. Independent Publishing, 2016. EBook.

Champion, Laurie. "I Keep Looking Back to See Where I've Been:" Bobbie Ann Mason's "Clear Springs" and Henry David Thoreau's *Walden*. *The Southern Literary Journal*, vol. 36, no.2, 2004, p. 47. *Google Scholar*,

https://scholar.google.com/scholar?hl=en&as_sdt=0%2C5&q=%22I+Keep+Looking+Back+to+See+Where+I%27ve+Been%22%3A+Bobbie+Ann+Mason%27s+%22Clear+Springs%22+and+Henry+David+Thoreau%27s+%22Walden%22&btnG=, Accessed: 04-06-2020 07:37 pm

Chris R. Vanden Bossche. "Albion: A Quarterly Journal Concerned with British Studies." *Albion: A Quarterly Journal Concerned with British Studies*, vol. 34, no. 3, 2002, pp. 523–524. JSTOR, www.jstor.org/stable/4054787.

Clingerman, Forrest. "Review of *Remembering Places: A Phenomenological Study of the Relationship between Memory and Place*. Authored by Janet Donohoe. *Environmental Philosophy*, vol. 12, no. 1, 2015, pp. 121–123. *JSTOR*, www.jstor.org/stable/26169824, Accessed on 29 June 2021at 2.14 pm.

Collective Unconscious, *Encyclopaedia Britannica*, Encyclopaedia Britannica Press, 2020, https://www.britannica.com/science/collective-unconscious, July 09, 2020.

Cooper, Laurence D. "Nearer My True Self to Thee: Rousseau's New Spirituality – and Ours." *The Review of Politics*, vol. 74, no. 3, 2012,p. 472-474, *Google Scholar*, https://scholar.google.com/scholar?hl=en&as_sdt=0%2C5&q=Nearer+My+True+Self+to+Thee%3A+Rousseau%27s+New+Spirituality%E2%80%94and+Ours&btnG=, Accessed at 3.22 pm. on 09-09-2020.

Costandi, Mo. "Bipedalism, Birth and Brain Evolution." *The Guardian*, 7 May, 2012, https://www.theguardian.com/science/neurophilosophy/2012/may/07/1

Coverley, Merlin. *The Art of Wandering: The Writer as Walker*. Old Castle Books. 2012.

.... *The Art of Wandering: Writer as Walker* by Merlin Coverley and *Ways of Walking: Ethnography and Practice on Foot* edited by Tim Ingold and Jo Lee Vergunst.

.... *Psychogeography* by Merlin Coverley, Pocket Essentials Series.

Dean, Bradley P. and Gary Scharnhorst. "The Contemporary Reception of "*Walden*"". *Studies in the American Renaissance*, 1990, pp. 293-328, Joel Myerson, https://www.jstor.org/stable/30227595.JSTOR.

Drew, John. *The Uncommercial Traveller*. Orion Publishing Group, *Dickens' Journalism Volume IV: 'The Uncommercial Traveller' and Other Papers, 1859–70* (2000). Dickens Journals Online, The University of Buckingham,

2000.http://www.djo.org.uk/indexes/articles/the-uncommercial-traveller-iv.html

.... *The Uncommercial Traveller.* Orion Publishing Group, *Dickens' Journalism Volume IV: 'The Uncommercial Traveller' and Other Papers, 1859–70* (2000). Dickens Journals Online, The University of Buckingham, 2000. https://www.djo.org.uk/indexes/authors/charles-dickens/the-uncommercial-traveller.html

.... Charles Dickens' "Uncommercial Traveller" Papers (1860-69): Roots, Interpretation and Context. 1994. Birkbeck College, PhD dissertation,

British Library EThOS: Search Results (bl.uk). Accessed on 22-08-2020, 12.20 pm.

Eliot, T. S. "Hamlet and His Problems." The Sacred Wood. 1919. Reprinted in *Writing and Critical Thinking Through Literature*, eds. Heather Ringo and Athena Kashyap, *Libretexts,* 2019.

https://human.libretexts.org/Courses/ASCCC/Writing_and_Critical_Thinking_Through_Literature/6%3A_Literary_Criticism/6.3_Literary_Criticism_Readings/Eliot%2C_T.S._%22Hamlet_and_His_Problems%22_from_The_Sacred_Wood_(1919)

.... "The Waste Land." *Poetry Foundation,* 2020. https://www.poetryfoundation.org/poems/47311/the-waste-land

.... *Murder in the Cathedral.* Longman Study Edition, Faber and Faber, 1935, pp.56.

Elkin, Lauren. "Flaneuse-ing." *Flâneuse: Women Walk the City in Paris, New York, Tokyo, Venice, and London.* Kindle, Penguin Random House, 2016.

Eva, Brann et al., Introduction, *Phaedo* by Plato, Focus Publications, 1998.

Fairclough, Norman. "Language in New Capitalism." *Discourse and Society,* Vol. 13, No.2, Mar. 2002, pp. 163-166. Editorial.

Falk, Dean, et al. "Metopic Suture of Taung (Australopithecus Africanus) and its Implications for Hominin Brain Evolution", *PNAS*, Vol. 109, No. 22, pp. 8467-8 470, https://doi.org/10.1073/pnas.1119752109.

Fischer, Barbara and Philipp Mitteroecker. "Covariation Between Human Pelvis Shape, Stature, And Head Size Alleviates The Obstetric Dilemma." *PNAS*, May 5, 2015, https://www.pnas.org/content/112/18/5655.

Fletcher, Angus, and Harold Bloom. *Allegory: The Theory of a Symbolic Mode.* Princeton University Press, 2012.

Ford, Lida. "A Great and Spherical Zero: Creative Works." *Department of Comparative Literature*, Robert D. Clark Honors College, June 2020, Thesis, https://scholarsbank.uoregon.edu/xmlui/bitstream/handle/1794/25746/Final_Thesis-Ford_L.pdf?sequence=1&isAllowed=y

France, Peter. Introduction. *Reveries of the Solitary Walker*, by Jean-Jacques Rousseau, Penguin, 1979.

Franz, Marie-Luise von. *C.G. Jung: His Myth in Our Time Studies in Jungian Psychology by Jungian Analysts*, Translated by William H. Kennedy, Inner City Books, 1998, p.105.

Freud, Sigmund. *Beyond the Pleasure Principle.* Translated and edited by James Strachey, W.W. Norton & Company, 1961.

.... On Freud's "Beginning the Treatment." Edited by Christian Seulin and Gennaro Saragnano, Karnac Books, 2012.

.... "Dream Work." Cultural Theory and Popular Culture: A Reader. Edited by John Storey, University of Sunderland, Person, 2006. Google Books. https://books.google.co.in/books?id=jgav8surlTIC&pg=PR3&source=gbs_selected_pages&cad=3#v=onepage&q&f=false

.... Standard Edition of the Complete Psychological Works of Sigmund Freud: An Infantile Neurosis and Other Works. Volume XVII, Translated by James Strachey et. al, London: Hogarth Press, 1917-1919.

https://uncanny.la.utexas.edu/wp-content/uploads/2016/04/freud-uncanny_001.pdf, Accessed on 4 May 2021 at 8.30 am.

.... The Civilization and Its Discontents. First Edition, Translated and Edited by James Strachey, Norton, 1962, PDF. p.19n14,

http://w3.salemstate.edu/~pglasser/Freud-Civil-Disc.pdf.

Golding, William. *Lord of the Flies: A Novel.* New York: Perigee, 2006.

Gourevitch, Victor. 'A Provisional Reading of Rousseau's "Reveries of the Solitary Walker."' *The Review of Politics.*Vol. 74, No. 3 2012, pp. 489-518. https://www.jstor.org/stable/23263386?seq=1#page_scan_tab_contents

Gros, Frederic. *A Philosophy of Walking.* Translated by John Howe. Verso, 2014.

Gruss, Laura Tobias and Daniel Schmitt. "The Evolution of the Human Pelvis: Changing Adaptations to Bipedalism, Obstetrics and Thermoregulation." NCBI, 2015, https://www.ncbi.nlm.nih.gov/pmc/articles/PMC4305164/, Accessed on 10-12-18, 5.38 pm.

Hegel, G. W. G. *Phenomenology of Spirit.* Translated by A. V. Miller, Oxford University Press, 1977.

"Hermeneutic circle." *Oxford Reference.* Accessed on 25 Jul. 2021 at 05.47 p.m. https://www.oxfordreference.com/view/10.1093/oi/authority.20110803095932789

Hewes, Gordon W. "Food Transport and the Origin of Hominid Bipedalism 1." *American Anthropologist*, Vol. 63, No. 4, 1961, pp. 687-710. *Google Scholar*, https://scholar.google.co.in/scholar?hl=en&as_sdt=0%2C5&q=Food+Transport+and+the+Origin+of+Hominid+Bipedalism1&btnG=, Accessed on 26/07/ 2021 at 12.15 pm.

Hollington, Michael. "Dickens the Flâneur." *Dickensian,* vol. 77, no. 394 1981, p 71. *ProQuest*, https://www.proquest.com/openview/aab957b1b8f8207ada53dfda54d7f8a2/1?pq-origsite=gscholar&cbl=1818261, Accessed at 5.31 pm. on 12-12-2020.

Horkheimer, Max and Theodor W. Adorno. *Dialectics of Enlightenment: Philosophical Fragments.* Edited by Gunzelin Schmid Noerr, Translated by Edmund Jephcott, Standford University Press, 2002. Print.

"Irony." *Fowler's Dictionary of Modern English Usage.* Oxford University Press, 2015.

Iyer, Pico. "The Deadman Walking," *Flights into the Foreign.* Vintage, 2005.

Ingold, Tim, and Jo Lee Vergunst, eds. *Ways of Walking: Ethnography and Practice on Foot.* Ashgate Publishing, Ltd., 2008. *Google Scholar,*

https://scholar.google.com/scholar?hl=en&as_sdt=0%2C5&q=Ways+of+Walking%3A+Ethnography+and+Practice+on+Foot+Anthropological+studies+of+creativity+and+perception&btnG=

.... Abstract of "Footprints through the Weather-World: Walking, Breathing, Knowing." *The Journal of the Royal Anthropological Institute*, vol. 16, 2010, pp. S121-S139. *JSTOR.*

"Joseph Brodsky". "The Editors of Encyclopaedia Britannica." *Encyclopaedia Britannica,* n.d, https://www.britannica.com/biography/Joseph-Brodsky. Accessed 11 June 2021

Jung, C. G. "The Stages of Life." *Structure and Dynamics of the Psyche,* Translated by R. F. C. Hull, edited by Herbert Read et al., vol. 8, Princeton University Press, 1975, pp. 240, 244-45.

.... "The Stages of Life". *Structure and Dynamics of the Psyche,* Translated by R. F. C. Hull, edited by Herbert Read et al., vol. 8, Princeton University Press, 1975, pp. 365. https://www.jungiananalysts.org.uk/wp-content/uploads/2018/ 07/C.-G.-Jung-Collected-Works-Volume-8_-The-Structure-and-Dynamics-of-the-Psyche.pdf. *JSTOR.*

Kaas, John H. "The Evolution of Brains from Early Mammals to Humans." *NCBI,* Nov 8, 2012, *U.S. National Library of Medicine,* https://www.ncbi.nlm.nih.gov/pmc/articles/PMC3606080/, Accessed on10-12-18, 5.38 pm.

Ko, Kwang Hyun. Origins of Bipedalism. *Brazilian Archives of Biology and Technology,* Vol. *58,* No.6, pp.929-934, 2015, https://doi.org/10.1590/S1516-89132015060399 www.jstor.org/stable/40606068. Accessed 24 Apr. 2021.

Lacan, Jacques. *The Four Fundamental Concepts of Psycho-Analysis.* Translated by Alan Sheridan, Edited by Jacques-Alain Miller, Penguin Books, 1977.

.... *The Four Fundamental Concepts of Psycho-Analysis.* Translated by Alan

Sheridan, Edited by Jacques-Alain Miller, Penguin Books, 1977.

Lane, Joseph H. "Reverie and the Return to Nature: Rousseau's Experience of Convergence." *The Review of Politics,* Vol. 68, No. 3, 2006, pp. 474-499, Cambridge University Press, https://www.jstor.org/stable/20452803.

Lane, Joseph H. and Rebecca R. Clark. "The Solitary Walker in the Political World: The Paradoxes of Rousseau and Deep Ecology." *Political Theory,* vol. 34, no. 1, Feb. 2006, pp. 62–94, doi:10.1177/0090591705279076. *Sage Journals.*

https://journals.sagepub.com/doi/abs/10.1177/0090591705279076#articleCitationDownloadContainer

Leisman, Gerry, et al. "Thinking, Walking, Talking: Integratory Motor and Cognitive Brain Function." *NCBI*, 2016, Vol. 4, No. 94, https://www.ncbi.nlm. nih.gov/pmc/articles/PMC4879139/.

Leys, Ruth. *Trauma: A Genealogy*. University of Chicago, 2000.

Livant, Bill. "The Dialectics of Walking on Two Legs". *Science & Society*, Vol. 62, No. 3, Dialectics: The New Frontier, 1998, pp. 414-416, Guilford Press Stable, https://www.jstor.org/stable/40403731, Accessed: 31-05-2019 10:33 am.

Lovejoy, C. Owen. "Evolution of Human Walking". *Scientific American*, Vol. 259, No. 5, 1988, pp. 118-125, *JSTOR, http://www.jstor.org/stable/24989268.*

Mackenzie, Hazel. *'Allow Me to Introduce Myself – First, Negatively:' Charles Dickens, Anthony Trollope, William Makepeace Thackeray and First-Person Journalism in The 1860s Family Magazine*. Sep.2010. Department of English and Related Literature. PhD Dissertation. University of York.

British Library EThOS: Search Results (bl.uk)

Man, Paul de. 'Sign and Symbol in Hegel's "Aesthetics,"' *Critical Enquiry*, Vol. 8, No. 4, 1982, pp.761-775. University of Chicago Press, http://www.jstor.org/stable/1343196,

Man, Paul de. 'Sign and Symbol in Hegel's "Aesthetics,"' *Critical Enquiry*, vol. 8, no. 4, 1982, pp.761-775. University of Chicago Press, http://www.jstor.org/stable/1343196

McElligott, Anthony. Editor, *The German Urban Experience: Modernity and its Crisis, 1900-1945*, Routledge, 2001, Digital Edition, 2005. p. 209. EBook.

Monteiro, George. "Redemption Through Nature: A Recurring Theme in Thoreau, Frost and Richard Wilbur." *American Quarterly*, Vol. 20, No. 4, Winter, 1968, pp. 795-809, The Johns Hopkins University Press, https://www.jstor.org/stable/2711409, Accessed: 26-05-2019 05:15. JSTOR.

Newton, Richard. "Travel and the World, Walking." *Goodreads*, 1 May 2013, https://www.goodreads.com/book/show/13369533-the-old-ways

Accessed on 08-06-2021 at 10.58 pm.

Nicholson, Geoff. *The Lost Art of Walking*. Riverhead Books, 2008.

Nixon, Rob. "Paths of Enlightenment." *The New York Times*. 7 Dec. 2012.

https://www.nytimes.com/2012/12/09/books/review/the-old-ways-by-robert-macfarlane.html, Accessed on 09-06-2021 at 08.58 am.

Olivelle, Patrick. *The Asrama System: The History and Hermeneutics of a Religious Institution*. Oxford University Press, 1993. Print.

Orwell, George. *1984*. Secker and Warburg, 1949.

Parkhill, Thomas. "Going to the Forest: The Case of the Pāndavas." *Annals of the Bhandarkar Oriental Research Institute*, 1986, Vol. 67, No. 1/4, pp. 133-138 http://www.jstor.com/stable/41693241 *JSTOR*.

Quinn, Arthur. *Figures of Speech: Sixty Ways to Turn a Phrase*. Routledge, 2010.

Ringel, Shoshana and Jerrold R. Brandell. *Trauma: Contemporary Directions in Theory, Practice, and Research*, Sage Publications, 2012,

https://www.amazon.com/Trauma-Contemporary-Directions-Practice-Research/dp/141297982X, Accessed on 06-08-19, 6.45 pm.

Rousseau, Jean-Jacques. "Discourse on the Origin and Foundations of Inequality among Men or Second Discourse," *The Discourses and Other Early Political Writings*, translated by V. Gourevitch, Cambridge: Cambridge University Press. p.187, 1997. *Google Books*. https://books.google.co.in/books?id=wZrFPXXhZ90C&printsec=frontcover&source=gbs_ge_summary_r&cad=0#v=onepage&q&f=false

.........*The Confessions* (1782), translated by J. M. Cohen, London, Penguin, 1953, p. 382.

Skoyles, John R. "Human Balance, the Evolution of Bipedalism and Dysequilibrium Syndrome." *Medical Hypotheses*, 2006, vol. 66, pp. 1060–1068. *Oxford Dictionary of English*, Third Edition, 2010.

"reification." *Oxford Reference. Oxford University Press.* Date of access 28 Jun. 2021, https://www.oxfordreference.com/view/10.1093/oi/authority.20110803100412880

Ringel, Shoshana and Jerrold R. Brandell. *Trauma: Contemporary Directions in Theory, Practice, and Research.* Sage Publications, 2012,

https://www.amazon.com/Trauma-Contemporary-Directions-Practice-Research/dp/141297982X, Accessed on 06-08-19, 6.45 pm.

Scott, David. *Rewalking Thoreau and Asia: 'Light from the East 'for' a Very Yankee Sort of Oriental." Philosophy East and West,* vol. 57, no. 1, 2007, pp. 14-39, University of Hawaii Press, URL: https://www.jstor.org/stable/4488074, *JSTOR*.

Skoyles, John R. "Human Balance, the Evolution of Bipedalism and Dysequilibrium Syndrome." *Medical Hypotheses*, 2006, Vol. 66, pp. 1060–1068.

http://evolution.binghamton.edu/evos/wp-content/uploads/2010/01/Harcourt-Smith-Aiello-2004.pdf

"This is the Scientific Reason Why Childbirth Has Always been so Painful and Extremely Dangerous," *Wittyfeed: Beyond Stories*, 7Apr. 2019, https://m.dailyhunt.in/news/india/english/wittyfeed+india-epaper-witty/this+is+the+scientific+reason+why+childbirth+has+always+been+so+painful+and+extremely+dangerous-newsid-66119414,

Accessed on10-12-18, 5.56 pm.

Seal, Bobby. "Baudelaire, Benjamin and the Birth of the Flâneur".*Psychogeographic Review*, 14 Nov. 2013, http://psychogeographicreview.com/baudelaire-benjamin-and-the-birth-of-the-flaneur/, Accessed on 31-03-18 at 9.45 pm.

Seale, Kirsten. "Eye-swiping London: Iain Sinclair, Photography and the Flâneur." *Literary London: Interdisciplinary Studies in the Representation of London*, Vol 3, No. 2, September 2005, http://www.literarylondon.org/london-journal/september2005/seale.html. Accessed on 05-07-21 at 11.03 am.

Shakespeare, William. *Macbeth.* Edited by Barbara Mowat, Paul Werstine, Michael Poston, and Rebecca Niles. Folger Shakespeare Library, June 29, 2021, p. 53, https://shakespeare.folger.edu/search/?search_text=wolf,

Accessed on 29-06-2021 at 12.45 pm.

.... *Macbeth. New Cambridge Shakespeare, Edited* by A. R. Braunmuller,

Cambridge University Press, 1997. EBook.

.... *King Lear. The Folger Shakespeare.* Ed. Barbara Mowat, Paul Werstine, Michael Poston, and Rebecca Niles. Folger Shakespeare Library, p.173, p. 137, https://shakespeare.folger.edu/shakespeares-works/king-lear/act-4-scene-1/,

Accessed on 12 July 2021 at 5.09 p.m.

.... *King Lear.* Edited by Burton Raffel, *Annotated Shakespeare*, Yale University Press, 1987, EBook, p.174

Schwartz, Susan L. *Rasa: Performing the Divine in India,* Columbia University Press, 2004.

Shaya, Gregory. "The Flâneur, the Badaud, and the Making of a Mass Public in France, circa 1860-1910." *The American Historical Review*, vol. 109, no. 1, 2004, pp. 41–77. *JSTOR*, www.jstor.org/stable/10.1086/530151.

Shields, Rob. "Fancy footwork Walter Benjamin's Notes on Flânerie." *The Flâneur*, Edited by Keith Tester, Routledge, 2015.

"Siddha." *Yogapedia*, June 12, 2018, https://www.yogapedia.com/definition/5361/siddha, Accessed on 22-09-2021 at 5.37pm.

"Sirius." The Editors of Encyclopaedia Britannica. *Encyclopaedia Britannica*, n.d.,

"Joseph Brodsky." The Editors of Encyclopaedia Britannica, n.d., n.p. https://www.britannica.com/biography/Joseph-Brodsky. Accessed 11 June 2021

Skillen, Anthony. "Rousseau and the Fall of Social Man." *Philosophy*, vol. 60, no. 231, Jan., 1985, pp. 105-121, *Cambridge University Press*, https://www.jstor.org/stable/3750565, Accessed: 11-04-2020 10:43. *JSTOR*.

Solnit, Rebecca: *Wanderlust: A History of Walking.* Penguin Books, 2000. Chapter 1, EBook.

Stein, William Bysshe. "The Motifs of the Wise Old Man in Walden." *Modern Language Notes*, vol. 75, no. 3 Mar., 1960, pp. 201-204, *The Johns Hopkins University Press*, https://www.jstor.org/stable/3040533, Accessed: 26-05-2019 03:10. *JSTOR*. Review.

Stephen, Bijan. "In Praise of Flâneur." *The Paris Review*. 17 Oct 2013, https://www.theparisreview.org/blog/2013/10/17/in-praise-of-the-*flaneur*/, Accessed on 31-03-18 at 9.20 pm.

Summers-Bremner, Eluned. "Reading, Walking, Mourning: W. G. Sebald's Peripatetic Fictions". *Journal of Narrative Theory*, Vol. no. 34, No. 3, 2004, pp. 304–34. https://muse.jhu.edu/article/186849, Accessed on 21-04-16 at 9.00 am.

Susan Buck-Morss, "The Flâneur, the Sandwichman and the Whore: The Politics of Loitering," *New German Critique*, Vol. no. 39, No. 2, pp. 99-140. *JSTOR*, http://www.jstor.org/stable/488122, Accessed on 16-12-2014 at 7.20 pm.

Sword, Helen. *Stylish Academic Writing*. Harvard University Press, Cambridge, 2012.

"This is the Scientific Reason Why Childbirth Has Always been so Painful and Extremely Dangerous," Wittyfeed: Beyond Stories, 7Apr. 2019, https://m.dailyhunt.in/news/india/english/wittyfeed+india-epaperwitty/this+is+the+scientific+reason+why+childbirth+has+always+been+so+painful+and+extremely+dangerous-newsid-66119414, Accessed on10-12-18, 5.56 pm.

Thurschwell, Pamela. *Sigmund Freud*, Routledge Critical Thinkers: Essential Guides for Literary Studies, Routledge, London, 2001, EBook, p. 85-86, 104.

"Transcendentalism." *Oxford Dictionary of English*, Third Edition, 2010.

Trocchia, Robbie. "We in Space: Wandering in the Work of Valeria Luiselli." Vassar College, Mar 2014, https://digitalwindow.vassar.edu/cgi/viewcontent.cgi?referer=&httpsredir=1&article=1349&context=senior_capstone

Tyler, Daniel. "Introduction", Uncommercial Traveller, Oxford University Press, 2015.

Valmiki. "Balakanda," *Sloka and Translation*, *The Ramayana*. Sarga 1, IIT Kanpur, nd. Web. Accessed on 28 Aug. 2020 at 9 am. https://www.valmiki.iitk.ac.in/sloka?field_kanda_tid=1&language=dv&field_sarga_value=1

Vyasa, Krishna-Dwaipayana. *The Mahabharata*, Book 7: *Drona Parva*, "Abhimanyu-badha Parva," translated by Kisari Mohan Ganguli, Section 33, *The Mahabharata Online*, https://www.mahabharataonline.com/translation/index.php, Accessed on 26-08-2021 at 9.44 am.

Wayman, Eric. "Becoming Human: The Evolution of Walking Upright." *smithsonian.com, August 6, 2012*, https://www.smithsonianmag.com/science-nature/becoming-human-the-evolution-of-walking-upright-13837658/. Accessed on 15/08/2018 at 1.15 pm.

……… "What Chimps Could Tell Us about How Humans Started Walking on Two Legs." *smithsonian.com*, March 26, 2012, https://www.smithsonianmag.com/science-nature/what-chimps-could-tell-us-about-how-humans-started-walking-on-two-legs-165505625/, Accessed on 15/08/2018 at 1.15 pm.

Werkley, Caroline E. "Eiseley and Enchantment." *Prairie Schooner*, University of Nebraska Press, vol. 61, no. 3, Fall 1987, pp. 60-63 https://www.jstor.org/stable/40636351, Accessed: 04-06-2019 08:04 pm

Weston, Daniel. "The Spatial Supplement: Landscape and Perspective in W.G. Sebald's *The Rings of Saturn*." Cultural Geographies, vol. 18, no. 2, Apr. 2011, pp. 171–186, doi:10.1177/1474474010397596.

Wylie, John. "A Single Day's Walking: Narrating Self and Landscape on the South West Coast Path." *Transactions of the institute of British Geographers* 30.2 (2005): 234-247. *Google Scholar*, https://scholar.google.com/scholar?hl=en&as_sdt=0%2C5&q=john+wylie+walking&oq=John+Wylie, Accessed on 03-06-2019 at 05:48 pm.

Videos

Kissin, Evgeny. *Classical Epiphany - Classical Masterpieces* "Plato's Academy - Raphael's Painting: A Who's Who?" 14 Jan. 2018. *TheWords Wise Podcast.* https://www.youtube.com/watch?v=PQJb4OcSIAo Accessed on 17-12-2017 at 9.00 am

Tyler, Daniel. *Oxford Academic*, Oxford University Press, "What can *The Uncommercial Traveller* tell us about Dickens?" 6 Oct. 2015, https://youtu.be/WC7Dlyxmxow

.... "Where did the persona of the 'uncommercial traveller' originate?" *Oxford Academic*, Oxford University Press, 6, Oct. 2015, https://www.youtube.com/watch?v=nYDPpX0O8VU, Accessed on 16-12-2017 at 8.00 pm

Index